Managing Organizational Risk Using the Supplier Audit Program

Also available from ASQ Quality Press:

Advanced Quality Auditing: An Auditor's Review of Risk Management, Lean Improvement, and Data Analysis
Lance B. Coleman, Sr.

The Certified Supplier Quality Professional Handbook
Mark Allen Durivage, editor

The ASQ Auditing Handbook, Fourth Edition
J.P. Russell, editor

Proactive Supplier Management in the Medical Device Industry
James B. Shore and John A. Freije

The ASQ Supply Chain Management Primer
ASQ's Customer–Supplier Division and J.P. Russell, editor

Quality Risk Management in the FDA-Regulated Industry, Second Edition
José Rodríguez-Pérez

The ISO 9001:2015 Implementation Handbook: Using the Process Approach to Build a Quality Management System
Milton P. Dentch

The Certified Six Sigma Yellow Belt Handbook
Govindarajan Ramu

Handbook of Investigation and Effective CAPA Systems, Second Edition
José Rodríguez-Pérez

Practical Design of Experiments (DOE): A Guide for Optimizing Designs and Processes
Mark Allen Durivage

Quality Risk Management in the FDA-Regulated Industry
José Rodríguez-Pérez

The Certified Pharmaceutical GMP Professional Handbook, Second Edition
FDC Division and Mark Allen Durivage, editor

Failure Mode and Effect Analysis: FMEA from Theory to Execution,
Second Edition
D. H. Stamatis

Managing Organizational Risk Using the Supplier Audit Program

An Auditor's Guide Along the International Audit Trail

Lance B. Coleman, Sr.

ASQ Quality Press
Milwaukee, Wisconsin

American Society for Quality, Quality Press, Milwaukee 53203

Printed in the United States of America
24 23 22 21 20 19 18   5 4 3 2 1

Library of Congress Cataloging-in-Publication Data

Names: Coleman, Lance B., Sr., 1962– author.
Title: Managing organizational risk using the supplier audit program : an auditor's guide along the international audit trail / Lance B. Coleman, Sr.
Description: Milwaukee, Wisconsin : ASQ Quality Press, [2018] | Includes bibliographical references and index.
Identifiers: LCCN 2018006191 | ISBN 9780873899680 (hard cover : alk. paper)
Subjects: LCSH: Materials management. | Risk management. | Auditing, Internal.
Classification: LCC TS161 .C595 2018 | DDC 658.7—dc23
LC record available at https://lccn.loc.gov/2018006191

ISBN: 978-0-87389-968-0

ASQ Mission: The American Society for Quality advances individual, organizational, and community excellence worldwide through learning, quality improvement, and knowledge exchange.

Attention Bookstores, Wholesalers, Schools, and Corporations: ASQ Quality Press books, video, audio, and software are available at quantity discounts with bulk purchases for business, educational, or instructional use. For information, please contact ASQ Quality Press at 800-248-1946, or write to ASQ Quality Press, P.O. Box 3005, Milwaukee, WI 53201-3005.

To place orders or to request ASQ membership information, call 800-248-1946. Visit our website at http://www.asq.org/quality-press.

ASQ
Quality Press
600 N. Plankinton Ave.
Milwaukee, WI 53203-2914
Email: books@asq.org
Excellence Through Quality™

This book is, first and foremost, dedicated to my beautiful wife of over 31 years, Lorraine. You graciously put up with all the foibles inherent in living with a continuously improving, lean thinking, quality engineering, comic book reading, auditor-for-life kind of husband. You remain both my love and my inspiration. Next, to the newest addition to our family, my wonderful grandson Sheldon Kenneth Johnson Jr. Truly, the best is yet to come. I also want to dedicate this book to my children from birth—Larissa, Lauren, Lance Jr., and Latrice—as well as to my adoptive children, Sheldon Sr. and Veronica. A parent's greatest wish is for happy, healthy children that have an expanded worldview, with the potential to do more and to be *more. You, my children, have granted me that blessing. And last, but not least, I dedicate this book to my two dogs, Leo and Shii, for always making my return home a cause for celebration, even on the worst of days.*

Table of Contents

List of Figures and Tables

Preface

Risk elimination. Risk management. Risk mitigation. These terms are an increasingly important part of the lexicon of executive-level management as they strive to succeed in a business environment having global competition, geographically diverse suppliers, and new technologies. In this new, globally expansive marketplace, more than 50 percent of value creation is achieved outside of an organization's walls, or, in other words, through their suppliers. This, too, is where the majority of product realization risk lies. This book will help clearly define what risk-based thinking is and how to apply it from the perspective of helping manage organizational risk through the supplier audit process. Suppliers are increasingly global in nature, which makes understanding cultural nuance more important than ever in building successful customer–supplier relationships. The chapter on international auditing will provide a comparison between conducting domestic and international audits, as well as an understanding of how to successfully incorporate cultural understanding into supplier audit planning and execution.

Read on to learn how a robust supplier audit program can help manage organizational risk, and what role supplier audits *should* play in the supplier approval process. Join our discussion on conducting a successful supplier audit and how to identify, assess, and mitigate risk in the work environment. Auditing tips, tools, and techniques, along with practical application of various risk assessment tools, will be shared. You will also learn how to conduct a risk-based supplier audit. Finally, readers will learn how the incorporation of various improvement and quality tools into the audit process can produce results that will also minimize organizational risk while helping to optimize organizational performance. For those transitioning from first-party to second-party auditing, the difference between supplier and internal auditing will be explored. A glossary of important auditing terms is also included.

The book is divided into two sections plus a conclusion and appendix. The first section explores supplier management, supplier auditing, and the supplier audit process. The second section discusses the skills, both traditional and nontraditional, needed to ensure a successful supplier audit. Relevant aspects of the ASQ Certified Quality Auditor and Certified Supplier Quality Professional bodies of knowledge will be discussed in detail. Individual chapters contain relevant quotations, highlight key thoughts to understand, and share cases in point that illustrate important themes while providing tips on how to handle the various unusual situations that an auditor might come across when conducting supplier audits anywhere throughout the world.

Finally, I am thrilled to have friends and colleagues from around the globe sharing their own stories in conjunction with mine in crafting the "Case in Point" vignettes interspersed throughout the book. Thanks to them, some of the industries reflected within these pages include medical device, logistics, automotive, and aerospace. Tales from Canada, Kenya, and throughout the United States are included. This book is meant to provide a detailed and useful discussion of the practical application of risk-based supplier auditing principles. It is also intended to be a primer for those new to the profession of supplier auditing, and to share tips and best practices that would benefit experienced auditors as well. These pages represent experience gained while conducting hundreds of domestic audits as well as audits conducted in six countries around the world over the course of a 20-plus-year career in auditing. I have tried to "leave nothing on the table." I hope that you enjoy reading this work as much as I have enjoyed writing it.

Acknowledgments

I would like to acknowledge my friends and colleagues James Metto, Kristen Wagner, Janet Bautista Smith, Denis Devos, Sheronda Jeffries, and Shauna Wilson for taking time out of their busy schedules to contribute to the cases in point shared in the following pages. I would also like to acknowledge my friend and colleague Duke Okes for his support, for many engaging conversations on the latest and greatest in auditing, as well as for our collaboration on the development of new and unique training materials on the very important topic of risk-based quality auditing. Also, thanks to my friend and Six Sigma mentor Jim Boblett, who is a constant resource when it comes to understanding Six Sigma tools, methods, and uses. Any mistakes that I may have made in discussing the application of these tools will certainly be due to my own stumbles in understanding. I have to give a nod to the ASQ Audit Division, which, for over 26 years, has been setting the standard and constantly raising the bar internationally for what it means to be considered a professional auditor and for what it means to conduct a good audit. I am proud to be a member of your leadership team. I would like to thank Alexa Druckmiller for providing her editorial skills to assist me in presenting as polished a work as possible to Quality Press for their consideration. Lastly, I would like to thank my managing editor, Paul O'Mara, for his shared vision and support of this project in addition to the editorial efforts of his team in partnering to craft what I hope you will agree is a very readable and value-added work.

Introduction

To understand how supplier audits can help manage organizational risk, you must first understand where the supplier auditing process fits within the overall supply chain management system. The American Production and Inventory Control Society (APICS) provides the following definitions of supply chain and supply chain management:

- *Supply chain.* The global network used to deliver products and services from raw materials to end customers through an engineered flow of information, physical distribution, and cash. (*APICS Dictionary*, 15th Edition)
- *Supply chain management.* The design, planning, execution, *control*, and *monitoring* of supply chain activities with the objective of creating net value, building a competitive infrastructure, leveraging worldwide logistics, synchronizing supply with demand, and measuring performance globally. (*APICS Dictionary*, 15th Edition)

Control and monitoring of suppliers is where said auditing comes in. Review and analysis of supplier audit results is an important part of driving improvement and managing risk.

Why is the control and monitoring of suppliers so important? Often, more than 50 percent of value creation is achieved outside of the walls of an organization. In fact, almost 100 percent of manufacturers here in the United States have at least one aspect of their finished product created outside of their walls. With this being the case, there is huge organizational risk existent within the supply chain that must be well managed. Weaknesses within the supply chain can lead to quality problems, delivery issues, or both. Recent industry trends have shown regulators enforcing greater control over suppliers by manufacturers for these reasons. If you require further justification, look to the news. Over the course of the past five years there have been multiple instances where supply chain concerns have made international news. Here are several of the most notable examples:

- 2016: Samsung recall of its Galaxy Note 7 due to fires resulting from lithium-ion batteries sourced from a supplier that provided 60 percent of the batteries used.
- 2016: Toyota recalls over 23.1 million vehicles worldwide due to malfunctioning Takata airbag inflators, whose malfunction has been linked by authorities to over 16 deaths internationally.
- 2013: European horse meat scandal where certain products advertised as being beef contained up to 100 percent horse meat.
- 2012: Tsunami offshore of Japan that disrupted supply chains worldwide for months.

Supply chain risk can manifest itself in the form of compromised consumer safety, product liability, tarnished business reputation, or a combination of these. In these few cited examples, you see safety issues due to product failure, problems caused by mislabeling (horse meat is not harmful to humans), and delivery issues caused by a natural disaster.

A basic model of the supply chain system from the perspective of the finished goods manufacturer is shown in Figure I.1, depicting delivery of components and raw materials from suppliers, transformation into finished goods by the manufacturer, and delivery to the end user.

To demonstrate how a supply chain functions, the Council of Supply Chain Management Professionals (CSCMP) has developed the SCOR (supply chain operations reference) model, which divides the system into five phases, as shown in Figure I.2.

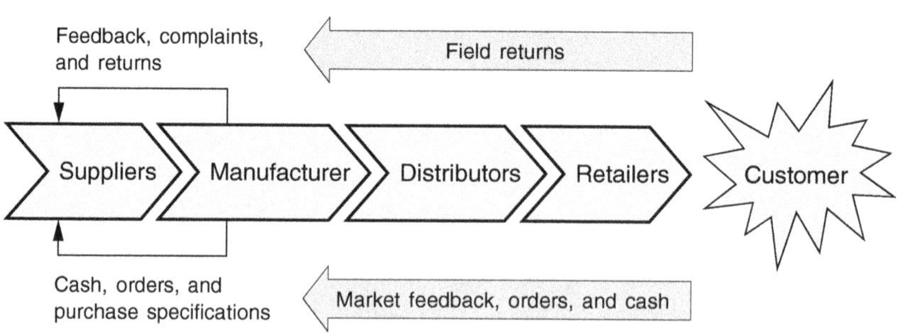

Figure I.1 Supply chain system model.

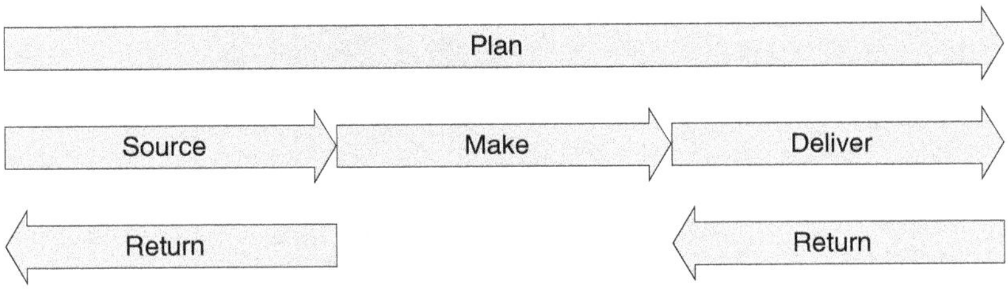

Figure I.2 SCOR model.

1. *Plan.* Planning to allow for balancing of supply with demand, communicated throughout the supply chain.
2. *Source.* The procurement of goods and services to meet demand. This includes identifying, selecting, and measuring performance of sources of supply, as well as delivering and receiving materials.
3. *Make.* Taking raw materials and components and transforming them into finished products having value for the end user.
4. *Deliver.* Providing resources to move materials along the supply chain from suppliers, to manufacturing, to customers. This includes order management, warehousing, and shipping.
5. *Return.* The reverse logistics process for product or material that is returned, including for repair, maintenance, and overhaul.

The ASQ Customer–Supplier Division body of knowledge (BoK) presents the *supplier life cycle management model* shown in Figure I.3. This model provides an integrated approach. It considers business and quality needs of the organization while also taking into account business and quality risks. Additionally, it is different from other models in that it explicitly considers reevaluation and decommissioning of suppliers as well.

The functional areas included within this definition of the supply chain system are information management, procurement, inventory flow scheduling and control, transportation systems and infrastructure, distribution facilities management, quality, and customer service (including order management and fulfillment).

As with other parts of a quality management system, supply chain management begins with the crafting of an organizational vision: What is our role in the marketplace? What are our values? Where do we see ourselves heading in the future? Blanchard and Stoner, from their 2011 book *Full Steam Ahead!*, identify three key elements of a compelling vision:

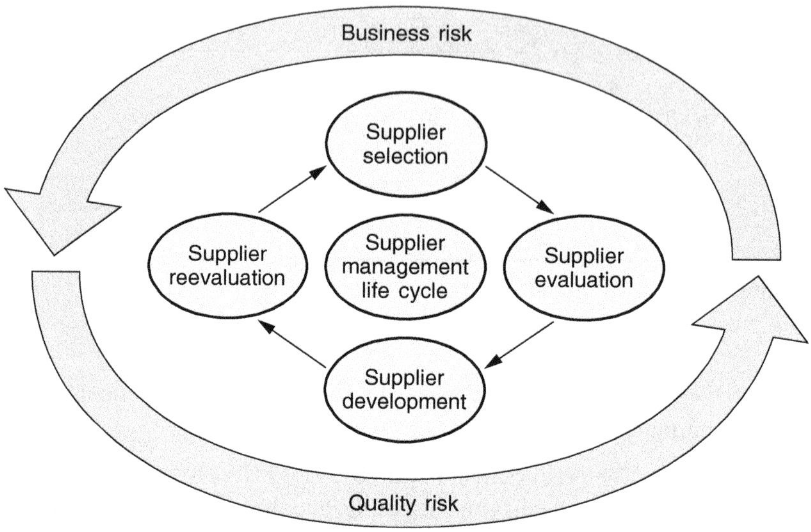

Figure I.3 Supplier life cycle management model.

1. Significant purpose
2. A picture of the future
3. Clear values

All three are needed to promote a common cause, clear and consistent direction, and motivation when times become difficult (and they will). From there, on a tactical level, a mission statement is developed that will support the strategic vision. Then strategies are developed that will allow for successful completion of the mission. That will break down silos and provide a road map for how organizational functions, such as information management, procurement, inventory flow scheduling and control, transportation systems and infrastructure, distribution facilities management, quality, and customer service, will collaboratively work together. Assuming the consistent requirement of a certain minimum level of quality, potential strategies that might be employed for supply chain management are low cost, quick turnaround/delivery, leading technology, compatible values, six sigma quality, or combinations of these and other factors. The strategies implemented will determine how risk tolerant the organization is. Operationally, suppliers would be selected, and then controls and monitoring put in place based on the overall strategy being deployed. Let us look at some examples:

- *Strategic vision.* Become a leading company worldwide; provide technologically advanced products that will help protect the environment.

  The sector that this company is working within is manufacturing and technology. They want to establish leadership in their market globally, not just nationally. Their corporate values relate to protection of the natural environment. They plan to use cutting-edge technology to achieve their goals.

- *Mission statement.* Establish mutually beneficial relationships with all suppliers, including those having new and unique products and technologies that will help this organization provide cutting-edge products that help preserve the environment.

  This is an example of what I call a "closed loop" mission statement. The first part of the mission statement pertains to the purpose of the supply chain management program, while the second half of the statement describes how this purpose supports the overall corporate vision. The benefit of this type of mission statement is that it "closes the loop" by prompting the organization to not just ensure that they are remaining on task, but to verify that successful implementation of the plan is moving the organization forward in the direction of the goals set by the organizational vision.

- *Strategy deployment.* Pursuing cutting-edge technology means that you are going to have to be more risk tolerant because new and, sometimes, unconventional suppliers may need to be included within the traditional mix. Additionally, new technology, while proven through validation and initial release, will not have the history of field data on which to base decisions, as would be the case with an established product.

  Controls, such as quality agreements, purchase specifications, surveys, audits, incoming inspection levels, performance triggers, and more, must take this increased risk into account.

It should be noted that supply chains exist both within and without an organization. Internal supply chains flow raw materials, components, and information through various processes, such as manufacturing, inspection, and testing, from the receiving to the shipping dock. They may consist of functions such as customer service, shipping and receiving, purchasing, production, and, finally, distribution to customers. Sound familiar? Another phrase for an internal supply chain is *value stream.*

There are three broad methods for assessing supplier capability (new) and performance (existing): surveys, audits, and sample inspection (AQL). The output of each of these processes is a *report*. Two important terms to be aware of when evaluating suppliers are *capability* and *capacity*:

- *Capability* is the ability to produce product that consistently and predictably meets requirements.
- *Capacity* is the ability to meet customer demand *and* the agility to ramp up to meet increased future demand as required.

Onboarding (setting up) a supplier is part of the control process. The following are typical risk-related questions to be considered when onboarding a supplier:

- Do we have a history with this supplier?
- Does this supplier need to be audited?
- Does this supplier require an on-site or desk audit or both?
- How often should this supplier be audited?
- Should scheduled audits be on-site or desk audits or both?
- What is the AQL for this supplier's product?
- How do we monitor and analyze supplier performance?
- What is our action trigger?

Supplier performance monitoring expectations should be communicated to the supplier up front and should consider both tangible and intangible factors. It should also be noted that, while risk is attached to both, it could be more easily overlooked when considering intangibles.

Tangibles:

- Quality
- On-time delivery
- In-full delivery
- Audit results
- Supplier corrective action requests issued

Intangibles:

- Easy to work with

- Responsive to questions or concerns
- Open and forthcoming with information

The examples that I have provided for both supplier onboarding and performance monitoring are meant to be exemplary rather than exhaustive. As you see, though, the supplier audit process is an important part of both supplier control and monitoring. Factors such as audit type, audit frequency, and audit team complement are derived using fact-based decisions driven by risk. So far, we have talked about supply chain management and how the supplier audit program can help manage risk that is inherent within a supply chain. Let us now discuss what, exactly, we mean by *risk.*

ISO 31000:2009 speaks to enterprise (business) risk and is meant to be applied across industries, in businesses of all sizes and types. ISO 31000:2009 defines *risk* as the effects of uncertainty on objectives. ISO 9001:2015 *Quality management systems—Requirements* defines *risk* as the effect of uncertainty. *Uncertainty* is as good a definition as any for risk. When you are uncertain, it is often because you lack knowledge. When you lack knowledge, there is a higher likelihood of failure when embarking upon a particular project or endeavor. Though risk can be defined many ways, depending on the source, it is consistently noted that risk has two primary components: the potential impact of an adverse event and the likelihood that the adverse event will occur. Risk, when realized, can negatively impact the consumer, the product, the business, or society as a whole. We will have a more detailed discussion on risk, risk management, and risk-based thinking in later chapters.

Proper classification of the supplier is crucial to determining the type and level of controls placed on them. One method of classification, cited in ASQ's *Certified Supplier Quality Professional Handbook*, is the *portfolio segmentation model* shown in Figure I.4, created by Peter Kraljic. Kraljic uses a two-by-two matrix as a means of placing suppliers into broad risk-based categories that allow an organization to institute similar controls on groups of suppliers based on the matrix quadrant that they fall within.

Kraljic's four broad categories of classification are listed below with an explanation of where and why they would fit on the matrix. Kraljic recommends the following purchasing approaches for each of the four product quadrants. So, where an organization places a supplier on the matrix will guide the purchasing strategy for that supplier.

1. *Strategic products (high profit impact, high supply risk).* High risk and high reward—these products deserve the most attention from purchasing managers. Options include developing long-term supply relationships, regularly analyzing and managing risks,

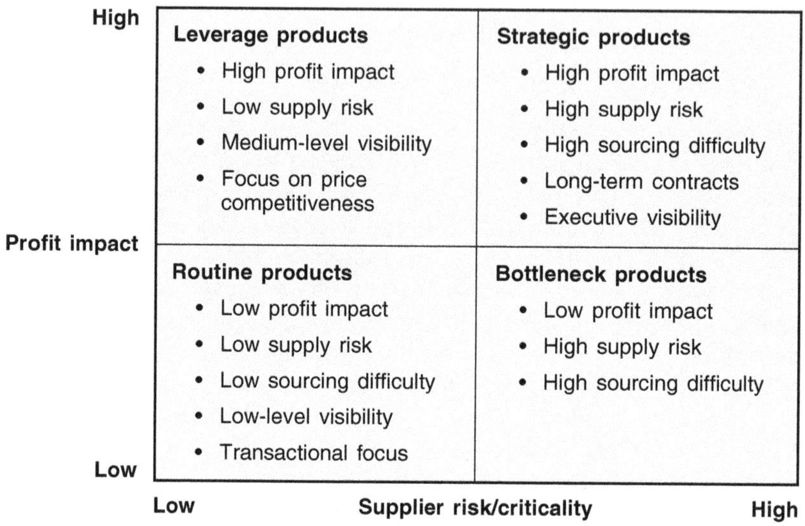

Figure I.4 Peter Kraljic's adapted portfolio segmentation model.

planning for contingencies, and producing the item in-house rather than buying it, if appropriate.

2. *Leverage products (high profit impact, low supply risk).* Purchasing approaches to consider here include using full purchasing power, developing alternative products or suppliers, and placing high-volume orders.

3. *Bottleneck products (low profit impact, high supply risk).* Useful approaches here include over-ordering when the item is available (lack of reliable availability is one of the most common reasons that supply is unreliable) and looking for ways to control vendors.

4. *Routine products (low impact, low supply risk).* Purchasing approaches for these items include using standardized products, monitoring and/or optimizing order volume, and optimizing inventory levels.

Now that we have covered the basics of supply chain management and understand supply chain risk, we will answer the question "What exactly do we mean by *audit* anyway?" Two regularly cited definitions across industries are:

- Systematic, independent, and documented process for obtaining *objective evidence* and evaluating it objectively to determine the extent to which the *audit criteria* are fulfilled. (ISO 19011:2018)
- A systematic, independent, and documented process for obtaining audit evidence and evaluating it objectively to determine the extent to which audit criteria are fulfilled. (*The ASQ Auditing Handbook*, Fourth Edition)

Philosophically, the supplier audit function is a vehicle for assessing whether or not an organization is meeting its obligations, both stated and implied. It should serve principally as a focusing lens on areas of nonconformity, but also as a compass for mutually beneficial continuous improvement and risk management efforts. Operationally, the purpose of the supplier audit function should be determined by the supply chain management strategy as a reflection of company or site needs, goals, and objectives.

The purpose of a supplier audit is to confirm three general things:

1. Continued (or assessed if new supplier) ability to meet product requirements
2. Continued (or assessed if new supplier) ability to meet production demands
3. Maintenance of an effective quality management system

Before we move on, it is important to point out that supplier auditing is not just about confirming compliance, or managing risk, or even improving performance. When done well, supplier auditing is also about building supplier relationships. Creating a positive relationship between the customer and supplier helps ensure that the product will be fit for use, with minimal corrective action and inspection needed. According to Joseph M. Juran, there are nine primary activities needed to achieve this goal:

1. Define product and program quality requirements
2. Evaluate alternative suppliers
3. Select suppliers
4. Conduct joint quality planning
5. Cooperate with the supplier during the execution of the contract
6. Obtain proof of conformance to requirements

7. Certify qualified suppliers
8. Conduct quality improvement programs as required
9. Create and use supplier quality ratings

Upon reflection, you will note that each of these nine primary activities requires aspects of planning, clear communication, relationship building, and risk management in order to be successfully realized. Looking ahead, we will begin to discuss in detail how the supplier audit program helps manage organizational risk, as well as the nuts and bolts of supplier auditing, in the next two chapters.

Part I

Supplier Auditing and the Supplier Audit Program

Chapter 1

Managing Organizational Risk Using the Supplier Audit Program

Planning for the supplier audit program begins with goal setting, which flows down from the organizational vision and corresponding mission statement. Goals for the supplier audit program should be set in order to (1) meet required metrics, (2) align with the corporate vision and related strategies, and (3) help drive continual improvement (both organizationally and within the supplier audit program itself). Goals should follow the SMART principle—specific, measurable, attainable, realistic, time-based.

The organizational vision, mission statement, and context of the organization within its chosen market all help determine how risk tolerant an organization will be. For example, an established company that is working within a mature market has plans to grow its market share through economies of scale and incremental improvements. Such a company would likely be more risk averse than a company looking to employ cutting-edge technology within its product and processes as a key differentiator.

Examples of key risk-related questions to address during the supplier audit program planning are:

- How is risk managed overall?
- How do we define risk?
- Is risk management well integrated into our supply chain business processes?
- What are the risks and rewards in going with a sole or single-source supplier?
- How do we incorporate risk management into audit planning?
- How do we look at audit results from the perspective of risk?

- Is our risk management strategy aligned with the organizational vision and mission?

A balance must be struck between risk tolerance and resource constraints. Do we have the resources to successfully implement our chosen strategy? Do we need to gather more resources or modify the strategy?

Some common controls that might be put in place based on supplier risk are quality agreements (quality assurance), quality management system audits (quality assurance), technological review (engineering), and financial/business overview (supply chain), as well as receiving inspection protocols (quality control) and performance monitoring (quality assurance/supply chain). You can see even by this partial listing that proper planning for supplier control is a cross-functional effort. It is also important to note that even those aspects of the control system that go into effect after suppliers have been brought online should be determined during the planning process.

What is the auditing philosophy of our organization? The context of the organization within its marketplace is often, and should be, a key driver in developing the audit philosophy. Operating with either new or mature technology, or within a mature or emerging market, will be determining factors. Remember that one definition of risk is "the effect of uncertainty." So, embracing the uncertainty of entering new markets and utilizing new technologies can lead to higher risk and should precipitate tighter controls, among which supplier audits would be included. Branding as best quality or best economics will be a determining factor regarding when to do supplier audits, as well as what type of audits will be conducted. What resources are available, both financial and personnel, to support the supplier audit program? The answers to these and other related questions will then allow the organization to structure the supplier audit program in answering these tactical-level questions:

- Are on-site audits a last resort until high risk dictates otherwise?
- Are on-site audits a given unless low risk dictates? A decision tree such as shown in Figure 1.1 can be developed and used to help make this determination in most cases. In those instances that still are not clear, a discussion between quality, supply chain, and key interested parties should be held to make a final determination.
- How prominent is the supplier audit program among the different supplier controls (receiving inspection and test protocols, quality agreements, supplier corrective action requests, and so on) that have been put in place? See the relationship between supplier audits and

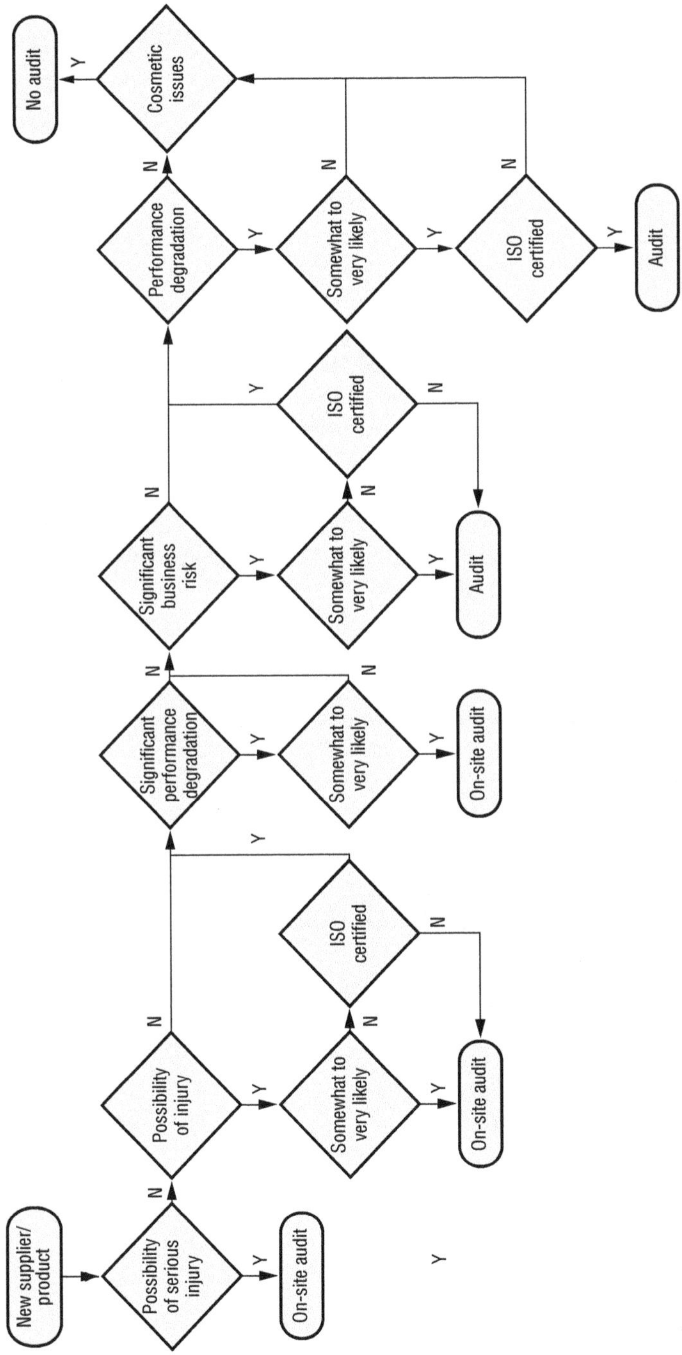

Figure 1.1 Supplier auditing decision tree.

other controls within the supplier management process in Figure 1.2.

It needs to be understood how we maintain a sightline with our organizational vision and build continual improvement into the DNA of our supplier audit program so that it helps drive us toward our desired future state. Another important factor for consideration is the development of standard work (practices). What technology platform (Excel, Word, iAuditor application, and so forth) do we use to generate audit working papers and otherwise support the supplier audit program? What types of audits will you do—system, process, product, element, or a combination of these, as appropriate? Are subject matter experts (SMEs) to be part of the audit team, meaning they would receive training as auditors? Or conversely, are SMEs primarily a support function with regard to the audit process, having a very specific role similar to administration or translation? Is our standard (default complement) one- or two-person audit teams? The consistency in both practice and appearance that comes with having standard work promotes efficiency and helps lend credibility to the audit program.

It is crucial to understand and clearly define the roles and responsibilities of the customer and supplier within the business relationship: who owns which responsibilities, and which, if any, responsibilities are shared? Ideally, there should be a baseline understanding or template(s) that can serve as a starting point for all quality agreements, but that can be built upon or revised as necessary to be specific to each supplier and the products that they provide.

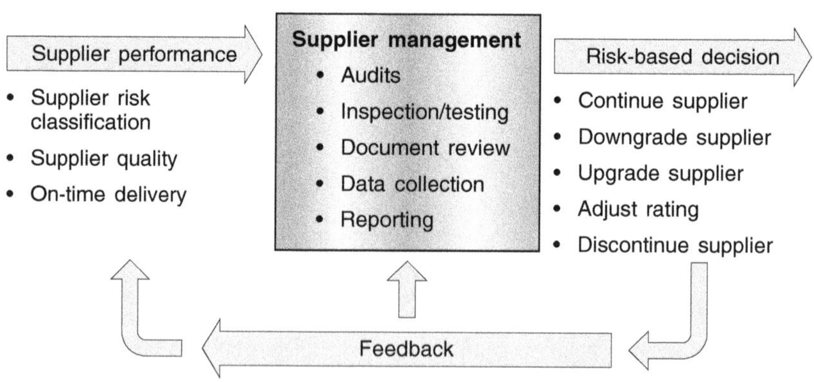

Figure 1.2 Supplier management process.

Supplier audit program planning needs to take into account three key elements—classification, response, and record keeping:

- *Classification*. Will you classify suppliers based on the highest risk of the products supplied—potential consumer risk, scarcity of the product they provide, business vulnerability, or some weighted combination of these factors?
- *Response*. What are the different levels of control that you put in place based on supplier classification? How are controls different during supplier setup and during performance monitoring of existing suppliers for the different classifications? What are our action triggers?
- *Record keeping*. What type of metrics should be tracked, which records should be kept, what medium should they be kept in, and for how long?

A periodic review of supplier audit program results against desired outcomes should be planned in order to determine acceptability of performance and whether or not goals need to be adjusted. Quantifiable metrics must be established to ensure a clear understanding among all interested parties as to what success looks like—both for the supplier and for the supplier audit program. It is important to sort this out beforehand because some supplier metrics and how you interpret them can be subjective. There is a very human tendency, when a supplier evaluation falls into the gray area of borderline evaluations, where the result is to take the "path of least resistance" and say, "this is okay." Notice that I *did not* say the "path of least risk." Having a clear understanding beforehand of what is and is not acceptable performance, in addition to what other factors should be considered in borderline cases, will help prevent this tendency to green-light a supplier that may require further reflection.

Two major pitfalls to avoid when planning the supplier management program are:

1. Going forward when there is a product that a company is desperate to have while there are quality management system, on-time delivery, financial, or other risks that would prompt a company with a mature quality management system to go forward only if they could put mitigations in place that would lower overall risks to an acceptable level. There is a reason, after all, that financial stability and business and quality systems, along with technical capability, are consistent considerations in evaluating suppliers. A mature organization might also try to form a relationship with

the supplier, if the supplier were willing, to help them develop to the point where the customer organization needs them to be. Otherwise, they would pass. No matter how desirable a new product or technology is, do not move forward with a supplier relationship unless you can mitigate any risks associated with the product, technology, or the supplier itself to an acceptable level.

2. Not having up front as clear as possible evaluation criteria as well as a structured and collaborative process for approving/disapproving suppliers that receive a marginal evaluation. Otherwise, unintentional bias may creep in for those suppliers that you "*really, really* want to use," for one reason or another, so that they are approved when they shouldn't be. This could mean having additional controls for suppliers receiving marginal evaluations, outright rejection of such suppliers, or some other response. How potential suppliers of important goods who have marginal evaluations are approved, disproved, onboarded, monitored, and controlled, shouldn't be left to chance.

Now let's look at how we develop an annual audit schedule. There are two principal things to take into account: needs and resources. For this scenario, let us assume that only high- and moderate-risk suppliers are audited, that low-risk suppliers are accepted based on ISO quality management system certification by an accepted registrar, and all suppliers must have an ISO quality management system certification.

First, ask your auditors the maximum number of audit days each is available for the year to determine the resources available. Plan for contingencies; take 90 percent of that number as your starting point. For example, you have 10 auditors and they can each give you six days per year. You have a total of 60 possible audit days. If you take 90 percent of that, you have 54 audit days. If we assume two days per audit, this allows for up to 27 audits with one auditor. If you wish to schedule two auditors per audit, you are now down to 13 possible audits, based on available resources. In actuality, the availability will vary from auditor to auditor, but for the sake of this example we will assume that all auditors have the same availability.

The next step is to look at the past three years and determine the average number of new supplier audits conducted. Let's say that number is four. You then have to set aside four audits to be determined (TBD) for the expected number of new supplier audits, which will leave you with the capacity to conduct nine planned audits of existing suppliers with your available resources. Following this process gives us a good sense of our capacity to conduct audits under optimal circumstances.

Separately, you have to determine which suppliers need to be audited based on risk and organizational procedures. First, you must identify which suppliers are due to be audited during the upcoming year as part of their (three-year, four-year, five-year, and so forth) cyclical rotation. Next, look at performance over the past year to see if any suppliers warrant being added to the schedule due to poor performance. This can be a first-time audit or possibly an audit that is moved up in the rotation to be performed a year (or more) early. Communicate with site management to inquire whether there are any suppliers that they may want to have audited for some other reason than poor performance (for example, considering them for new and/or different types of work).

Now that you know which suppliers need to be audited, you compare that with the number suggested by your available resources. If the need is greater than the resources, we can consider the following:

- Maybe two auditors aren't needed for every audit. If some audits have two auditors and some less complex audits only have one, we can increase the number of audits conducted.
- Remember that we identified resources based on 90 percent of maximum capacity. So, potentially, if everything goes as planned (and we know how often that happens), and we are able to audit at 100 percent of capacity, then that is another six possible audit days.
- Outside resources could be brought in, such as auditors from another company site, or contractors.
- Worst case, a determination could be made that there is low risk in pushing one or more audits back to the following year. This risk determination would likely be based on a combination of performance history and the product provided.

To go back to our example, let's say that 10 suppliers were due for auditing per their rotation, three suppliers need to be audited due to poor performance and inadequate response to supplier corrective action requests, and it is requested that two existing suppliers be added to the schedule because they are being considered to produce a very high-profile new component. All of this plus the four set-asides for new suppliers that need to be audited comprise the number of audits to be conducted. In this case we need to conduct 15 planned audits, while we have resources to conduct nine.

This reflects a shortfall of six audits or 12 audit days (six days auditing × two auditors per day). If we schedule at 100 percent of pledged capacity (60 audit days) instead of 90 percent, this gives us an additional six audit days. If we allow that six of the audits only require one auditor instead of two as is standard, then that will give us another six audit days. This is not an optimal scenario since six of the audits will only have one auditor and because we have pushed our resources to the maximum. However, we have managed to close the gap between what must be scheduled and available resources to conduct supplier audits for the year.

Suppliers added to the schedule due to performance issues should be scheduled earlier in the year, followed by suppliers designated as high risk, then those designated as moderate risk. Next, those audits tied to projects, product development, or product release should be scheduled in time to provide the required information to those requesting the audit.

We should also consider the true worst-case scenario in which a company does not want to allocate funding or resources to conduct any audits. In that instance you will need to make the business case for the audit. Research nonconformance reports to determine scrap, rework, and processing costs (cost of poor quality [COPQ]) attributed to the worst-performing suppliers. Research any instances within the past three (arbitrary time frame) during which there may have been an instance where poor supplier performance cost the company money. Present this information to management along with your proposed audit schedule and projected costs. If you can make the case that spending $20,000 in costs to conduct supplier audits might prevent $50,000 in losses down the line, as evidenced by recent history, management may be more likely to approve at least some level of on-site supplier auditing.

So, here you have my guidelines for how to develop an annual supplier audit schedule. Take what works for you, adjust as you see fit, and leave out what you don't need. This audit development process as described is not meant to provide step-by-step instructions to account for every circumstance, but rather to provide you with a helpful overview of the thought process that you go through to put together an annual audit schedule, the questions that should be asked, and the things to be considered.

Auditing is, by its very nature, risk managing. Some of the ways that we plan for and respond to risk, both within the supplier audit program structure and within individual audits, are to determine:

- Audit frequency
- Audit length
- Audit type
- Audit team complement
  - Who is the lead auditor?
- How experienced should auditors be?

  - How many auditors?
  - SMEs required?
  - Translator required?
- Audit complexity ([Number of auditors × Number of days] + Level of sampling)
- Follow-up audits (needed or not)

Increased value comes by formalizing this process. The consistent application of risk-based thinking throughout all aspects of the supplier audit program, from planning through implementation, is key to successful mitigation of the risks that come from outsourcing. Wait a minute, hold up—risk-based thinking? What is that? Here is what ISO 9001:2015 says about risk-based thinking:

> *Risk-based thinking enables an organization to determine the factors that could cause its processes and its quality management system to deviate from the planned results, to put in place preventive controls to minimize negative effects and to make maximum use of opportunities as they arise.* (ISO 9001:2015, 0.1 General)

This is a pretty detailed and clear-cut definition of risk-based thinking, isn't it? Well, if you reread the paragraph above, you see that it is *not.* What this ISO standard excerpt is really talking about are the benefits of employing risk-based thinking. It does not say what risk-based thinking actually *is.* In fact, after reading through both ISO 9001:2015 and ISO 9000:2015 and searching the Internet, I was surprised that there was no precise definition for risk-based thinking found in any internationally recognized source. I could find the definitions of *risk* and *risk management*, but not risk-based thinking. I then referred to ISO 14971 and ISO 31000, where I again saw definitions for risk assessment, risk management, and many other related terms, but not risk-based thinking. Hmmm . . .

It looks like we will just have to come up with our own definition!

Risk-based thinking is a matter of perspective in how we view the data and situations that we encounter and respond to each day. As we know, a *process* can be thought of as an activity that transforms inputs into outputs—in this case, perceptions and data. So, risk management can be thought of as an output (response) resulting from the application of risk-based thinking to the data, observations, and activities (inputs) that we encounter every day in the workplace, as shown in Figure 1.3.

To understand how you would apply risk-based thinking to data analysis, let's look at a scenario where a company has 20 suppliers that should

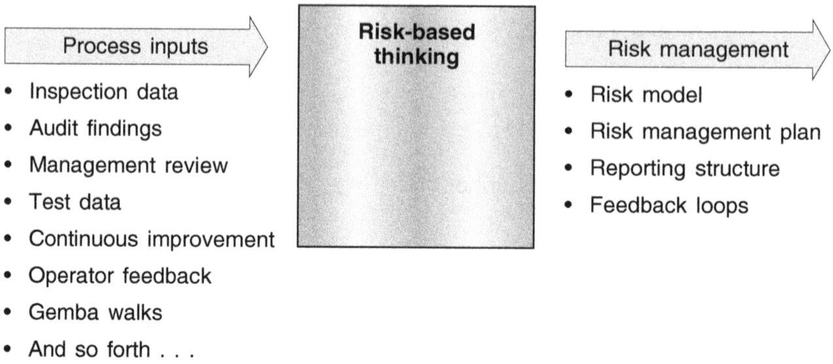

Figure 1.3 Risk-based thinking process map.

be audited this year according to the supplier auditing procedure, while only having resources to conduct twelve audits. You need to look at quality versus delivery and then process through multiple risk filters. Quality and on-time delivery (OTD) are selected for this scenario because they are the two most commonly used supplier performance metrics, in conjunction with other metrics. We will use a simple but effective prioritization tool to demonstrate risk-based thinking—the 2 × 2 matrix. You can put whatever you need to on the *x* and *y* axes in order to reflect the situation you are trying to understand. In this first case, we will place our suppliers A through T into a 2 × 2 matrix with quality on the *y*-axis and on-time delivery on the *x*-axis as shown in Figure 1.4. Once done, we see that we have four quadrants in the matrix reflecting the following conditions:

Quadrant I—No quality problems and no OTD problems

Quadrant II—No quality problems, but there are problems with OTD

Quadrant III—Quality problems and OTD problems

Quadrant IV—Quality problems but no OTD problems

The five suppliers in quadrant I are candidates to have their audits rescheduled. The five suppliers in quadrant III will definitely need to be audited. If a supplier is supposed to be audited per the long-range schedule and is having quality problems, then certainly they should be audited as well. Thus, the five suppliers in quadrant IV should also be added to the audit schedule. So, right now we have five audits that absolutely have to be done, five that should be done, and five that can be rescheduled.

Next we look at the five suppliers in quadrant II of Figure 1.4 with OTD issues but no quality problems. We place them on the 2 × 2 matrix (a business risk filter) seen in Figure 1.5. Do any of the suppliers provide product that if not available could affect customer delivery dates or multiple production lines? Looking at the matrix tells us that the two suppliers in quadrant III of Figure 1.5 pose a high business risk if parts become unavailable, so we add them to the audit schedule. The remaining three

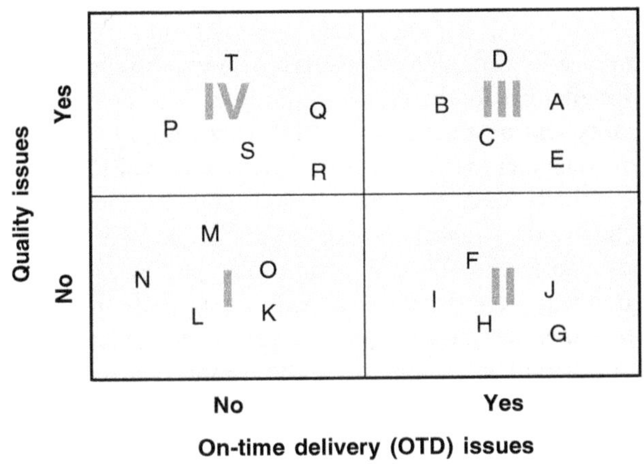

Figure 1.4 OTD issues versus quality issues.

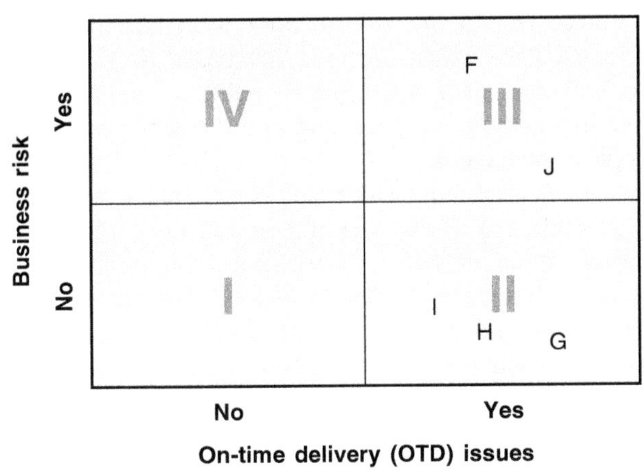

Figure 1.5 OTD issues versus business risk.

suppliers are candidates for rescheduling. The reason that I say *candidates* is that it is possible the company could acquire additional resources to close the resource gap that would allow them to audit all of the suppliers required within the year intended.

Now that we have arrived at a number of audits to be conducted that is in line with available resources, how would we prioritize them? First, those suppliers whose quality failures have either a 4 or 5 impact rating as defined in Table 1.1 should be prioritized. Then look at which failures have the highest *combined* impact and frequency of occurrence as defined in Tables 1.1 and 1.2. You will see in Table 1.3 the results of the prioritization.

To recap, we started out by considering how we might apply risk-based thinking to available supplier data pertaining to two key performance indicators—quality and on-time delivery. Then we reviewed the data through the lenses of consumer and business risk in order to make a fact-based decision on who to include on the audit schedule, and in what order they should be audited. Such a decision-making process helps the company manage risk and provides a defensible position when challenged by external auditors as to why certain suppliers were not audited as originally intended. It is very important to remember, however, that once it is demonstrated that there is low risk in rescheduling certain audits, the company must still demonstrate how they plan to recover. Otherwise, the same problem will reoccur the following year, now that eight scheduled supplier audits have been bumped back. This might mean converting some of the on-site audits for low-risk suppliers into desk audits (with justification), increasing available resources, or by some other means. If you are like me, then you rarely have all of the resources needed to accomplish *all* of the things you are tasked to do in the time allotted. That is why prioritization tools like 2 × 2 matrices are so helpful, particularly when applying risk-based thinking. Not only do they help visualize the data, but they also make a compelling statement, as opposed to a handwritten summary, when presenting your conclusions on whatever topic to management.

We just looked at applying risk-based thinking to supplier performance data. Now let's talk about how we might do the same with audit findings. Finding classification can be correlated to risk by combining the impact classifications as defined in Tables 1.1 and 1.2 with the frequency definitions shown in Table 1.3 for each audit finding; it is also possible by tying audit finding classification to risk level (see Table 1.4).

Another example of incorporating risk into finding classifications can be seen in Figure 1.6. In this instance, we use shading to designate the four levels of risk and then provide definitions for the four levels of impact and frequency that are combined to determine risk. The important thing to once again remember is that the levels of risk, the definitions, and even how

Table 1.1 Impact assessment.

Impact	1	2	3	4	5
Definition	Improperly completed forms and records (information still retrievable)	Failure to meet requirements that do not impact fit, form, or function	Failure that could lead to issues with form, fit, or partial malfunction. Failure that could cause significant business risk	Failure that could lead to significant or total malfunction of end product	Noncompliance that is itself a hazard or may lead to hazardous conditions, or cause harm or injury

Table 1.2 Frequency of occurrence assessment.

Occurrences	1	2	3	4	5
Definition	Fewer than 10% of lots or parts with issues	Between 10% and 20% of lots or parts with issues	Between 21% and 32% of lots or parts with issues	Between 33% and 50% of lots or parts with issues	Greater than 50% of lots or parts with issues

Table 1.3 Supplier audit priority list.

Priority	Supplier	Impact rating	Frequency rating	Overall risk rating
1	Supplier A	4	3	12
2	Supplier Q	5	1	5
3	Supplier P	4	2	8
4	Supplier C	3	4	12
5	Supplier F	3	4	12
6	Supplier D	3	3	9
7	Supplier E	3	3	9
8	Supplier J	2	4	8
9	Supplier T	3	2	6
10	Supplier S	2	2	4
11	Supplier R	2	2	4
12	Supplier B	3	1	3

Table 1.4 Risk level versus finding classification.

Risk	Finding classification
High	Major/critical
Medium	Minor/major
Low	Minor

risk is responded to should be defined in organizational procedures and be aligned with what has been determined appropriate by the organization.

Another method for taking risk into account when classifying audit findings is to assess the risk of failure against aspects of the quality management system based on the number and type of nonconformities identified within each area. For example, the sections of ISO 9001:2015 that would be assessed for risk are context of the organization, leadership, planning, support, operation, performance evaluation, and improvement. For a quality management system aligned with the Malcolm Baldrige framework, the aspects of the QMS assessed for risk would be leadership, strategy, customers, workforce, operations, results and measurements, analysis,

	Possible impact			
Frequency	**Negligible**	**Minor**	**Major**	**Critical**
Isolated incident				
Chronic				
Systemic				

Risk level	**Finding classification**
	Opportunity for improvement
	Minor noncompliance
	Major noncompliance
	Major noncompliance with need for intervention

Impact definitions	**Frequency definitions**
Negligible—An incident that has no product impact, an insignificant impact on operations, and, while it may be beneficial to improve, is not a violation of any kind.	*Isolated occasion*—One time or very infrequent occurrence. An occurrence that while possible, may never have occurred previously.
Minor—Violation of internal procedure or work instruction; Current practice that meets requirement is not accurately documented. Could lead to failure of part attributes. Isolated error.	*Chronic*—Issues or areas of concern that repeat over time. What is critical to understand is how often issues repeat and under what conditions.
Major—Violation of customer requirement or internal requirement. Systemic or chronic failure of QMS requirement. Multiple related minor viloations. Issue that could lead to failure of either finished good or part function or variables. Ethical violations. Issue that could cause great harm to other operations. Lost required record or procedure. Zero documented evidence of compliance. Direct violation of ISO standards or cGMP.	*Systemic*—Issues or areas of concern that repeat throughout different elements of the quality management or other organizational systems. Discovered during one time period over the course of a single audit.
Critical—Noncompliance that is itself a hazard or may lead to a hazardous condition. Issue that could directly lead to field failure of finished goods, potentially leading to injury of the end user. Legal violations.	

Figure 1.6 Finding classification risk matrix.

and knowledge management. Figure 1.7 shows examples of risk level classifications compared with aspects of the quality management system, based on audit findings.

In this case, it is not each individual audit finding that is assessed for risk, but rather the aggregate effect of all audit nonconformities related to a particular aspect of the quality management system and the risk of those nonconformities causing a failure in the system.

So, in thinking about how risk affects the classification of audit findings, we can look at the risk of individual nonconformities, the risk found within aspects of the quality management system, or the risk found within the overall quality management system (we can also directly audit the risk

Risk Level Definitions

A—Significant risk:

Potential for product contamination, complete product failure, or serious supply chain disruption.

Potential violation of customs/regulatory requirements or blatant disregard of technical/quality agreement.

Multiple systemic or chronic deviations from the requirements.

Conformity required within three months or according to agreement.

B—Moderate risk:

Required procedures do not exist, or exist but are not implemented or followed.

Lack of awareness or attention to cGMP requirements.

Lack of IT and other technical resources appropriate to the size of the business.

Deficient management systems for handling customer service, production planning, and inbound/outbound logistics.

Significant number of instances of partial fulfillment of requirements.

System is not achieving defined objectives.

Compliance required within six months or according to agreement.

C—Minor risk:

Regulatory, ISO, contractual, and internal requirements met in principle but not in full.

Current system needs additional focus and other improvements.

Compliance required within six months or according to agreement.

Figure 1.7 Risk level definitions for audit finding classification.

management program itself, as discussed in the next chapter). Finally, supplier audit program planning also takes into account risk when determining:

1. Audit frequency
2. Special training requirements for auditors
3. Complexity of individual audit plans
4. Minimum sample size required
5. Whether containment is necessary
6. The level of detail needed within corrective action plans
7. Effectiveness verification requirements

Thus far we have introduced the concepts of the supply chain and supply chain management. We have an understanding of how the supplier audit program responds to and helps manage risk. Now let's talk about what it means to conduct a risk-based supplier audit.

Chapter 2
Conducting a Successful Risk-Based Supplier Audit

Though our focus will be on risk-based supplier auditing, many of the tools and techniques discussed within this chapter would be beneficial in conducting any type of audit. As we will see below, the focus of a supplier audit can vary. Why, then, our emphasis on conducting risk-based supplier audits?

- *Compliance.* Do policies/procedures comply with requirements, and are they effectively implemented?
- *Performance.* Are desired/expected results being achieved by the QMS?
- *Risk.* What risks exist for which controls may not exist or be adequate? What risks are inherent to the quality management system?
- *Improvement.* What are some opportunities for improvement, and the risks associated with them?

When a supplier has a mature quality management system, it is unlikely that there will be major nonconformities. Management could begin wondering about the value of the audit program when only minor issues or opportunities are reported, becoming complacent and lessening support for quality initiatives. For the mature quality management system, the greatest opportunities will lie in managing risk to help drive improvement. Additionally, risk-based supplier auditing better protects the public (by helping manage risk), the customer, and the company as a whole. It leads to more-effective auditing and better management of limited resources, and makes for more efficient and effective processes. The four phases of any audit are planning, execution, reporting, and closure.

PLANNING

Now, before any audit planning can be done, authority to access the facility and conduct an audit must first be verified. This prevents wasting time in preparation for an audit that the supplier might not allow. Typically, the right to conduct audits is included within the contracts or quality agreements between supplier and customer. If this has not been done, an audit request can still be submitted to the supplier, but they will not be contractually obligated to comply. Two terms that are critically important in classifying the individual audit and that should be confirmed as the first steps in planning are:

- *Purpose.* The "what and why"—what are we doing, and why are we here? *Example:* "Confirm conformity of Supplier ABC quality management system to ISO 9001:2015 and Customer XYZ purchase specifications."
- *Scope.* The "where and when." *Example:* "The audit will take place at Supplier ABC in the Land of Oz on May 22, 2018, during first shift."

Along with confirming your authority to conduct the audit, the purpose and scope of the audit should be identified before any further audit planning takes place. A decision tree such as shown in Figure 2.1 can be used to help determine the audit team complement.

An important part of any audit, time management is even more critical when auditing suppliers. You typically don't get the chance to "come back to finish up" the next day. Managing your time during an audit starts with a well thought-out audit agenda. You will want to schedule a tour at the start of the audit in order to understand how work flows through the area(s) being audited. Limit the tour to 30 minutes, though. You don't want to take away too much time from the documented information review, interviews, and observations that take place during the rest of the audit. The rationale behind this practice is that during many supplier audits the audit team is only allowed to see processes in operation and records pertaining to product provided to the audit team organization. When possible, supplier audits should be scheduled when at least one of the auditing organization's processes is running, but this cannot always be accomplished. This may be due to the infrequency that certain jobs run, scheduling logistics, or lack of support from the supplier. When such is the case, you want to limit your tour to 30 minutes so that you can focus on audit evidence specific to your organization—records, documents, and overall quality management system effectiveness.

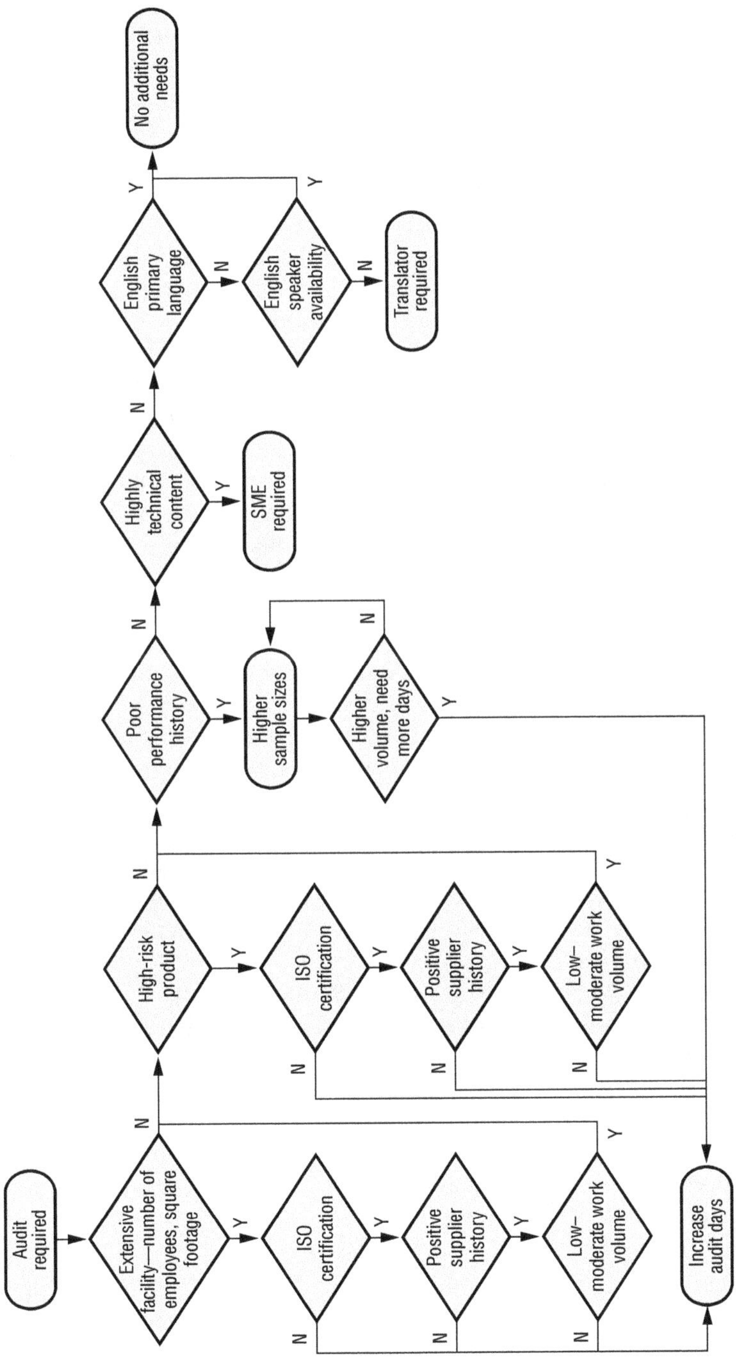

Figure 2.1 Audit team complement decision tree.

When you can arrange for one of your jobs to be running during the time of the audit, you can allow for up to 60 minutes for the tour in order to allow for time to ask more-detailed questions about the process and equipment where your job is running. Then you will want to schedule time to come back out on the floor later during the audit, possibly to conduct a process audit as part of the overall supplier audit. Plan to spend as much time as possible and as makes sense out on the floor where value is created. Having said that, it is important to find the balance that exists between being out on the floor observing, interviewing, and interacting with frontline employees and having enough time to thoroughly review relevant documents and records.

It is not necessary to follow the exact sequence of clauses of the criteria that you are auditing against on your schedule. However, you do want to start with an overview of the quality management system (for example, quality manual and quality policy) and leadership responsibility (leadership commitment, leadership communication, management review, and so forth). Then go over any nonconformities that need to be reviewed from the previous audit or any other items of concern (slipping performance, open supplier corrective action requests, for example). After that, organize the agenda in order to increase the likelihood of successfully reviewing all planned aspects of the quality management system. If there are areas where there often are no problems or that are easy and quick to review, move those toward the end of the schedule. That way if the audit team is running behind, they can either take smaller samples or perhaps skip a certain subclause with minimal risk of missing a significant nonconformance. Include an hour in the schedule before the closing meeting for audit team discussion and review of notes. This meeting is where the audit team reaches consensus on the classification of audit findings, and typically takes about a half hour. By scheduling an hour, you give yourself a 30-minute buffer that you can use if you are running behind. If the audit is on schedule, trust me, no supplier will complain if an audit ends 30 minutes early!

For an organization to function effectively, it needs to identify and manage numerous linked processes. The application of a system of processes within an organization—together with the identification and interactions of these processes, and their management to produce the desired outcome—is referred to by ISO quality management system standards as the "process approach." One important aspect of the process approach is conducting process audits. Now, how exactly do you conduct a process audit? The basics are pretty simple, actually:

- Confirm that all of the inputs are correct.
- Assess how the process is performing.
- Confirm that outputs are as expected.
- Compare output yields to other lines.

One example of how you would start a typical process audit would be to ask questions pertaining to the inputs based on the 6 M's—man, machine, material, method, measurement, and Mother Nature (environment):

- Man:
  - Operator knowledgeable of operation
  - Operator training records available
- Machine:
  - Equipment calibrated
  - Equipment maintained as required
  - Equipment correct
  - Settings correct
- Material:
  - Correct materials
  - Materials not defective
  - Required certificates (conformance, analysis, and so forth) available
- Method:
  - Operator actions match instructions
  - Instructions used are the most recent revisions
  - Instructions are correct
- Measurement:
  - Correct data being captured
  - Data capture done correctly

- Mother Nature:
  - Any environmental condition requirements met
  - Environment monitored
  - Safety and cleanliness evaluated
  - Line clearance effective

Next, you will assess how the process is performing and how it is being monitored:

- Performance:
  - Performing as expected
  - Gauge/meter readings as expected
- Monitoring:
  - Monitored as required
  - Data recorded as required
  - Data trending appropriately
  - Correct data being captured

Finally, a review of the outputs will take into account the following:

- Products:
  - Per specification
  - Yields as expected
  - Yields comparable to similar processes
- Records:
  - All required available
  - Completely filled out
  - Correctly filled out
- Signals:
  - Alerts, alarms, status signals sent as required
  - Sent alerts, alarms, and signals correct

- Consequences or risks associated with the overall process:
  - Properly mitigated

The type of process auditing where you follow the steps of a process from beginning through to the end is called *forward tracing.* An auditor could also start with the process outputs and work backwards. This method is referred to as *backward tracing.* You will notice in the process map in Figure 2.2 that one of the outputs of a process that should be considered is *risk.* Remember, for any activity that you are engaged in, there will always be some risks, however small. These could be risks of failure, injury, mistakes, and so forth. Now let's take a look at what happens when we shift the focus of the audit to risk.

How in-depth an audit is required to be depends on a combination of risk assessment, vulnerability of the organization, and performance history. Constraining factors are available resources and the level of accessibility to the supplier facility. The first step in planning for the audit is to determine what type of risk-based audit you wish to conduct. Risk-based quality audits can be thought of as having three levels:

- *Level 1.* Plan, audit, and report based on the risk found within each QMS process or within the QMS as a whole, as discussed in the previous chapter.
- *Level 2.* Evaluate the degree to which risk management is accomplished within QMS processes. To better understand the distinction between levels 1 and 2, risk-based audits let us look at the following scenario.

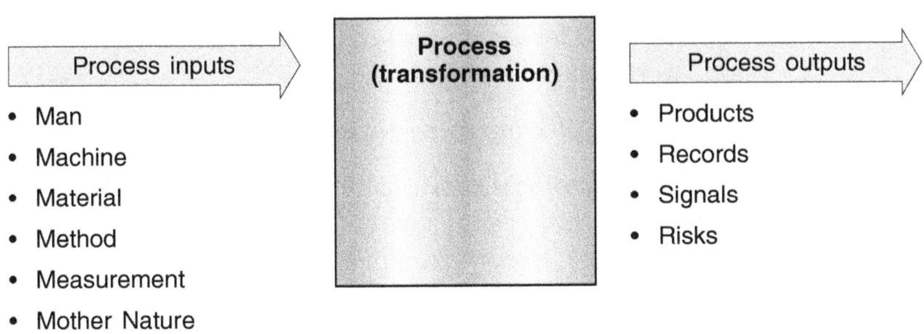

Figure 2.2 Process map.

Scenario: An auditor visits a machine shop and witnesses a welding operation where sparks are flying in the immediate vicinity. The operator is following their instructions and wearing the appropriate personal protective equipment (PPE), but the auditor notices a small puddle of oil on the floor nearby.

The hazards in this scenario are the sparks and the oil. The risks are those of slipping and falling, the sparks burning the worker, or the sparks catching the oil on fire. The key here is for the auditor to assess whether (1) all required controls (risk mitigations) are in place, and (2) whether they are adequate for the existing risks.

If the audit focus was on confirming conformity of this process, some of the questions to be asked might be:

- Is the operator performing the operation correctly?
- Do training records indicate that the operator has been trained on the latest revision of the relevant procedure?
- Do the parts being made meet requirements?
- Is equipment in the area calibrated and/or maintained as required?
- Are production records being properly completed and maintained?

If the audit focus was on performance or improvement, typical questions asked might be:

- Does the yield for this process meet expectations?
- How does the yield for the process compare across shifts, operators, work centers, and so forth?
- What opportunities for improvement are seen within the area?

An auditor might combine these different types of questions into one audit checklist where risk is a part of the evaluation, or do an audit where the sole focus is risk management, as opposed to level 1 risk-based supplier auditing where the focus is on verifying conformity and assessing the risk of quality management system failure, based on the identified nonconformities.

- *Level 3*. Determine enterprise- (business-) level risks related to QMS processes. In other words, based on the overall risks of failure of the quality management system, is there risk of negative impact on other integrated business systems? Alternatively, at level 3 the risk management program itself is audited.

When auditing the risk management program itself, you should seek to verify all of the following:

1. The program should encompass all aspects of the product life cycle from design to end-of-life disposal.
2. Data from external, as well as internal, sources should be captured and analyzed, and the risk model should be updated as necessary.
3. Teams, when formed, should be cross-functional in nature in order to model the broadest range of risks.
4. Confirm that results from the risk management program are reported as necessary to appropriate levels of management.
5. Confirm that existing risk management procedures and work instructions are followed.
6. Ensure that organizational training supports the risk management program. Top management, middle management, engineering, and hourly workers may all require different levels of training. However, all levels of the organization should be trained to some extent in risk management.
7. Ensure that periodic review and assessment of the need for a risk model update is embedded within the risk management program.
8. Confirm that adequate resources are supplied to meet the goals of the risk management program.

Once the authority to conduct the audit, and the audit purpose and scope, are confirmed, then planning can begin in earnest. Overall planning for the audit is accomplished by the lead auditor and should, as a minimum, address the items below. When there is only one auditor on the team, then that person is by default the lead auditor.

1. Review audit purpose, scope, and previous audit reports.
2. Develop a plan:
    - What type of audit are you conducting?
    - Implementation strategy.

- Resources needed.
- Logistics to address.

3. Determine the number of audit days.
4. Review regulatory and other external websites for any issues on the public record.
5. Communicate within and without the organization to identify any known or suspected performance issues.
6. Prepare audit assignments.
7. Communicate/coordinate with audit team.
8. Communicate/coordinate with auditee.

Once the planning is done and audit dates are confirmed with the auditee and the audit team, we then transition to the execution phase of the audit. Sometimes this phase of the audit is referred to as "field work."

EXECUTION

While on the tour it is okay to ask occasional questions for clarification that can be answered easily during the tour. It is also okay to ask if you can jot down equipment numbers and material identification during the tour so that you won't have to come back out on the floor during the calibration or material traceability portions of the audit. However, don't linger too long in one area or begin asking complex questions. You will typically be on a tight schedule when conducting a supplier audit. Asking in-depth questions begins to turn the tour into an ad hoc audit within the audit, which can disrupt the audit plan flow and possibly the schedule timeline. This could lead to not having time to review an important area. Remember, you can always come back out as necessary. Again, the exception to this rule would be when product supplied to your company is running on the line while the audit is being conducted. The amount of time spent on the floor should also be reflective of the complexity of the processes being audited. As a very broad rule of thumb, spend up to 15% of your time on the floor when your job(s) are not running and up to 50% of your time on the floor when your job(s) are running. Typically, once you have verified that there is a controlled procedure for records maintenance, the actual maintenance of records can be confirmed using the records that are looked at throughout the day while reviewing various aspects of the quality management system.

The key to managing time effectively is to be as efficient with time as possible while at the supplier's site. Review the schedule each hour to ensure that you remain on track and respond appropriately when you are falling behind. This may mean shifting assignments, reducing sample size, or even not auditing some aspect of the quality management system during the audit as planned. As a worst-case scenario, you could request certain records for review after you have left the site; keep this to a minimum, though, and understand that certain records will only be allowed to be reviewed while at the supplier's site.

The process approach espoused by the various ISO quality management system standards lends itself very well to managing risk. Before we dive in, though, let's review what we mean by a process. A *process* can be thought of as any activity that transforms inputs into outputs. In other words, some action has to be taking place; something has to be going on. A transformation also has to take place such that the items, materials, actions, methods, and so forth, that are put into the process are changed in some way and give something new and different as an output. Let's look again at the generic process map shown in Figure 2.2. In this instance, the possible inputs to a process are separated into the categories referred to as the 6 M's:

- *Man.* The actions taken by a human operator to initiate and/or facilitate the process.
- *Machine.* The equipment used during the process.
- *Material.* The raw material, components, and subassemblies that are going to be transformed.
- *Method.* The manner in which the operator is instructed to carry out their actions as indicated by standard operating procedures, work instructions, or through some other vehicle.
- *Measurement.* Any measurements or indicator readings that must be taken as part of the process.
- *Mother Nature.* The environment, such as any temperature, humidity, or cleanroom requirements; proper line clearance (all materials, documentation, and detritus from previous job removed from the work center); and lack of clutter in the area.

It has been found over time that most process inputs can be divided into these categories, though by no means is this the only way that you can classify inputs. Process inputs should be categorized according to what is most appropriate for the organization and the process under study. For outputs of a process, you have product (whether physical goods or some service), related documentation (completed forms/records), any identified process risks, and, when applicable, signals transmitted (that is, for computer or electronic systems).

To conduct a risk-based audit of a process, you will want to look at any risks inherent in the process inputs, the performance of the process itself, and the process outputs. Some of the risks that you would want to look for are the risks of nonconformity of raw materials and components, the process not performing as expected, operator error, test or inspection error, environmental issues, equipment failure, and so forth. In order to do that, you want to take the following steps:

1. Identify area hazards and risks.
2. Classify the hazards and risks.
3. Determine whether the risks are accounted for in the risk model.
4. Determine whether controls/risk mitigations are in place.
5. Determine whether controls/risk mitigations are adequate.

Scenario: A publishing company provides typographical services to their clients for the revision of their annual reports. The company job proposals include cost per hour and number of hours expected to complete the job based on the number of pages to be revised and the estimated number of changes per page. Runners deliver the work to work cells. Each work cell consists of two typists and two proofreaders, as shown in Figure 2.3. The process is as described below and shown in the process map in Figure 2.4, with inputs and outputs to each process step.

1. Individual pages are received with handwritten modifications.
2. Page recipient:

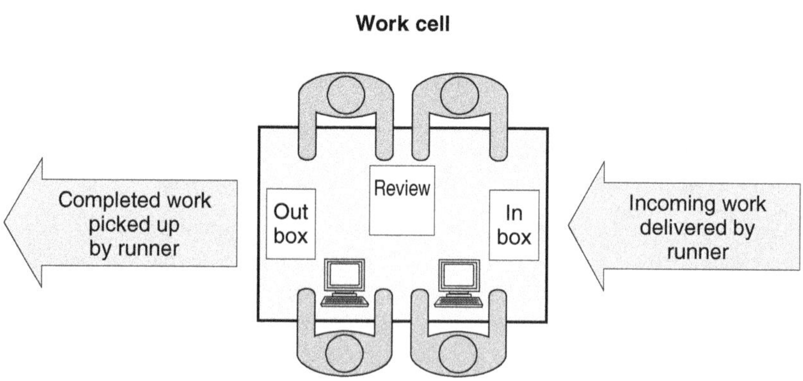

Figure 2.3 Publishing work cell.

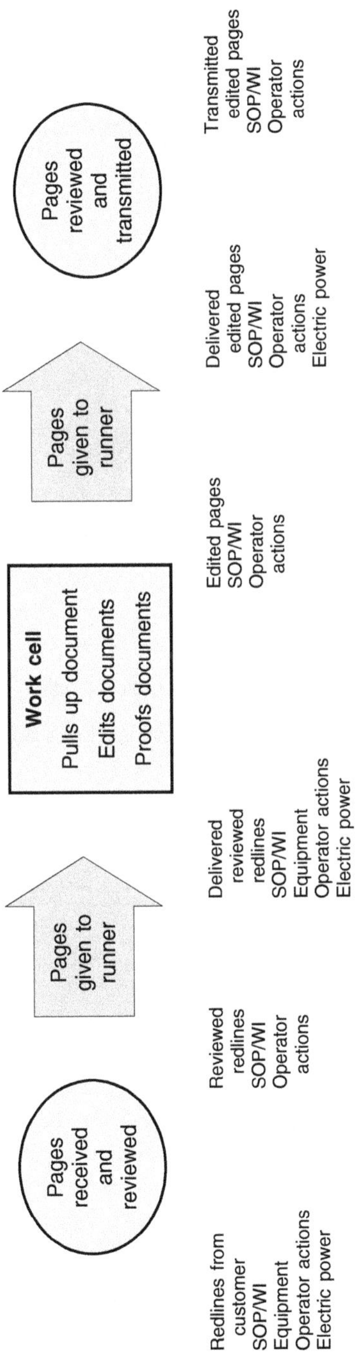

Figure 2.4 Document page revision process map.

   a. Verifies that the pages go to an active job
   b. Verifies that requested changes are legible
   c. Calls runner over and hands over pages for assigned work cell
3. Runner:
   a. Verifies which work cell pages go to
   b. Delivers pages to designated work cell in-box
4. Work cell:
   a. Typist:
      i. Pulls up document to be revised from SharePoint
      ii. Types in changes
      iii. Corrects any errors found by proofreader
   b. Proofreader:
      i. Proofs documents
      ii. Returns errors to typist for correction
      iii. Puts completed pages in work cell out-box
5. Runner:
   a. Picks up pages from work cell out-box
   b. Delivers pages to job planner
6. Job planner:
   a. Transmits document to customer

As you look at Figure 2.5 you will see that for every process step there are risks and hazards that could lead to either failure of that process step or failure of the overall process. Some are immediate while some are long term, but all should be addressed. Take note that for every hazard there is an associated risk, but the inverse is not true. You will also notice that the hazard of *poor lighting* is shared across each process step while the hazard of *old style keyboard* is only an issue within the work cell.

In Figure 2.6 you will see that various controls have been added to eliminate or mitigate certain risks and hazards. As an auditor, you will need to make an assessment when going through an area of whether or not controls are adequate to appropriately mitigate inherent process risks. You will

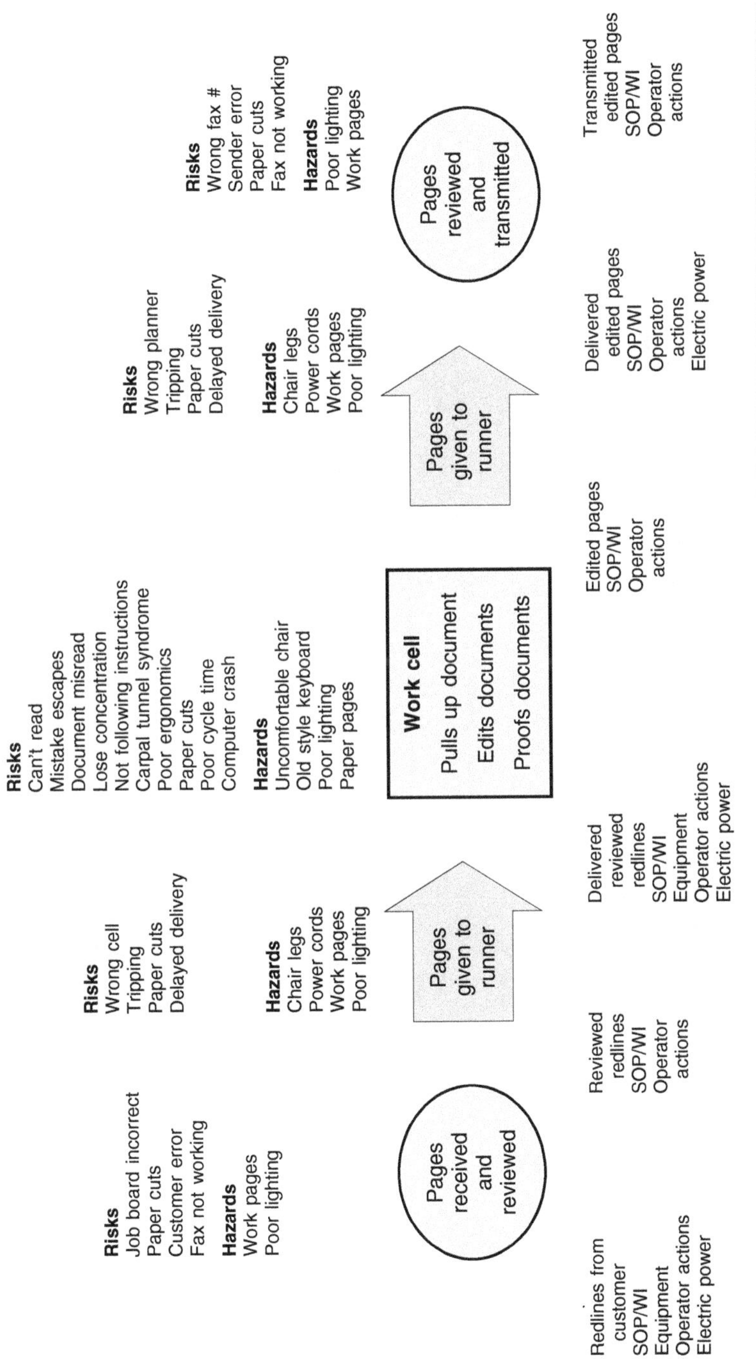

Figure 2.5 Document page revision process map showing hazards and risks.

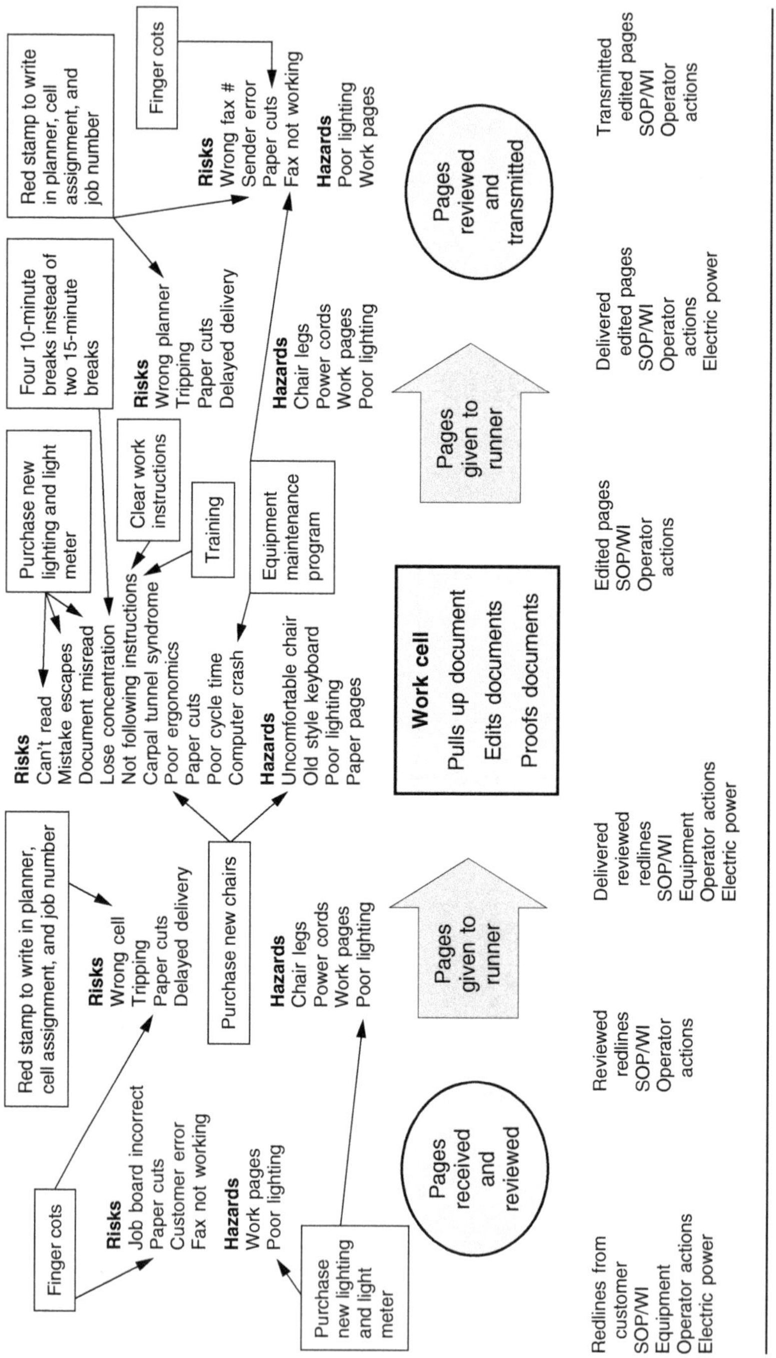

Figure 2.6 Document page revision process map showing hazards, risks, and controls.

also make a determination of whether there are any risks or hazards that have not been addressed. If so, then this may be considered either a nonconformity or opportunity for improvement based on the nature of the identified risks. How might you address the identified tripping hazard? What are some other risks/hazards that you see that should be addressed? How would you address those? If controls are found to be inadequate to address area risks, then this would be a nonconformity against the risk management program. If controls overall are adequate, but could be better, then these would be opportunities for improvement.

So what is the benefit of going through this type of exercise? When simply verifying compliance, there is a tendency to have "tunnel vision." "Procedures are being followed, training records are available, there are no 'red flags' jumping out at me, so we are good." However, an area can be conforming 100 percent to their procedure, but there may still be something important that was overlooked and is not addressed by the existing procedure. By opening their mind to try to identify every possible risk and hazard, and then assessing the controls in place to address each—of which the area standard operating procedure would be one—the auditor will often identify areas of concern that have been overlooked. The regulatory, ISO, and company requirements that preside over the area in question would then determine whether the oversight would be classified as either a nonconformity or opportunity for improvement. As stated earlier, this type of audit can be done as a stand-alone audit or as one aspect of a compliance or performance audit.

Note: For a more detailed description of this methodology across a more complex process map, look to the Risk Is the Compass model developed by Denis Devos in the 1980s and discussed briefly in my previous book, *Advanced Quality Auditing: An Auditor's Review of Risk Management, Lean Improvement, and Data Analysis.*

We have just taken the *process* approach to risk-based auditing. Now let's see how we would employ risk-based thinking when using the *elemental,* or *clause,* method of auditing.

When using the element method, the lead auditor should first assess the company documentation against the related clauses (elements) of the reference or external requirements. Any findings would then be against the supplier quality management system. Usually, this is done partially during a document audit that is part of the audit planning phase and partially on-site during audit execution.

Then auditors should compare employee actions and records (performance) against what is stated in their own internal documentation. Any findings noted would be against a lack of performance of actions as required. One way to think of this is that in step one you are validating that the quality management system functions as required. In step two you are verifying that, given the appropriate inputs (flowed-down requirements and documentation), the outputs (actions and results) are as expected. This approach is called the "W factor" and is depicted visually in Figure 2.7.

When a nonconformity breaches both an internal and an external requirement, then write one finding against the internal requirement but reference the external requirement. In other words, pull an excerpt from the internal document as the requirement, state what was observed, and then draw your conclusion. Reference the external requirement document number and relevant clause but not any of the language from the external document. The reason you would cite only one nonconformity in this instance is because you don't want to "double dip." Even though two requirements were violated, there is only *one* nonconformity. The reason that you will quote from the internal document requirement is that it is likely to be more detailed, more relevant to the company, and provide more information than the external source. The reason that you still want to reference the external source is to prevent the auditee from just stating as a corrective action that "we decided we don't need to do that" and changing the procedure. See Figure 2.8 for an example.

Findings can be classified as minor, major, or critical according to the risk classification of the individual finding as shown in Chapter 1 and Table 1.2 and Figure 1.8. Risk may also be determined according to the potential cumulative effects of the findings relating to a specific area of the quality management system. In the instance cited in Figure 2.8, the risk would be minor since this was the only finding of nonconformity against the

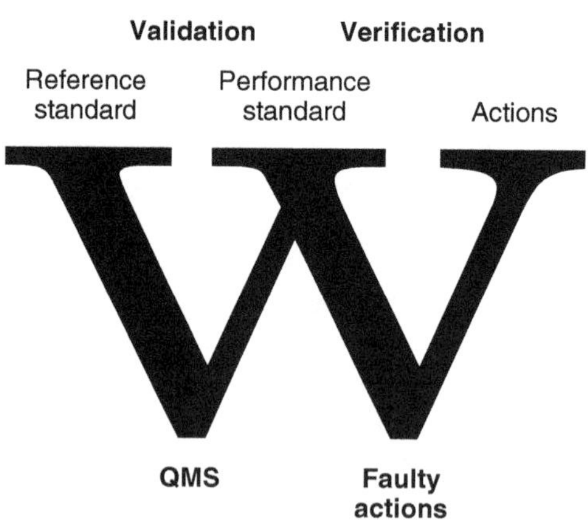

Figure 2.7 The "W" factor.

Source: Erik Myhrberg. Moorhill International. Used with permission.

Finding: AF-02	**Classification:** Minor noncompliance	**QMS reference:** Purchasing controls

Requirement:

PUR-001:5.3.1 (Revision D)—"Purchasing documents shall include, where possible, an agreement in which the suppliers, contractors, and consultants agree to notify the manufacturer of changes in the product or service so that manufacturers may determine whether the changes may affect the quality of a finished device." *External reference:* 21 CFR Part 820.50

What was observed:

- Purchase order supplier instructions do not include a requirement to inform supplier of any changes that may affect product quality.

Conclusion:

The requirements for purchasing controls are fulfilled in principle. This finding represents partial nonfulfillment of the requirement. Minor noncompliance.

Figure 2.8 Documentation of audit findings.

"purchasing controls" aspect of the quality management system. If chronic and/or systemic issues had been found, then the risk of failure of this aspect of the quality management system would have been elevated.

As mentioned previously, one key difference between supplier and internal audits is *transparency*. The vast majority of suppliers want to showcase their company and its processes, and so will be open and transparent. There are exceptions, however, when an auditor will receive intentionally misleading responses to their inquiries. There are also times when the data presented are suspect. Auditors need to recognize when this is the case. Studies have shown that we as humans communicate information following the pattern below:

- Body language 55%
- Vocal (tone) 38%
- Words 7%

Thus, it is key to not just hear *what* is being said but to listen for *how* it is being said. Also, look for any telltale body language cues. Two examples of behaviors to look out for when you believe there is information that an auditee representative may be intentionally hiding or misrepresenting are avoiding eye contact (though this could sometimes simply be a sign of nervousness) or changing behavior (for example, speaking louder, faster, or slower, looking away quickly before answering the question, faster blink rate than previously, and so forth). When you are unsure about a response, listen to your instincts and probe deeper. When reviewing reports and other data, be sure that you understand what success looks like when represented in a report or on a graph. Don't just accept "pass" or "accept" on an inspection or test report. Don't just accept a series of plotted data points that appear to be acceptable based on the image. Determine what the acceptable value range is for a sampling of criteria and verify that that the actual numbers incorporated within the report or plotted on a graph are truly passing.

While conducting the audit, whatever type it may be, it is important to remember that supplier audits are not just about confirming that the supplier is meeting requirements. Supplier audits are also an important part of building relationships. Auditors must always remember that they are the guests of the auditee. As such, they are bound by auditee rules while in the area, and should not touch, review, or copy anything or speak with anyone without first asking permission. Auditors should be fair in their presentation, follow site rules, and engage with the auditee in a polite and nonpunitive manner. Any deviation from acceptable behavior runs the risk of alienating the auditee, ruining rapport, and making it difficult to acquire the information and support needed in order to conduct a successful audit.

The communication established during the audit is a two-way street. As a supplier auditor, you should also be receptive to identifying any gaps in desired behavior on the part of your organization. Does your organization respond to inquiries or approval requests in a timely fashion? Does your organization communicate drawing and specification changes in an effective and efficient manner? Are you reasonable in your requests? Don't forget to bring back opportunities for your organization to better help the supplier. If you do identify things that your organization can do better to help the supplier, don't just put it in your report and forget about it; follow up to see if the issue was addressed or at least assigned to someone to look into as an action item. Such behavior will promote greater transparency from the auditee, increasing the likelihood of a successful audit and improved relations.

KEY THOUGHT

An auditor should not allow themselves to be unescorted in a work area for more than a few minutes. Being unescorted for too long can open the auditor up to potential liability and other issues.

Even when you behave as the perfect guest, conflict will occasionally arise. In order to keep an audit on track, and to maintain access to required information, conflicts must be resolved quickly and effectively. Conflicts can occur with the auditee or within the audit team itself. Conflict can be a significant risk to the successful completion of a supplier audit. There are different ways to handle conflict:

- *Avoiding* an issue or person is not an option if the conflict is relevant to the audit.
- *Smoothing over* may be an option if the issue is minor or irresolvable. Those in conflict should focus on what they agree on instead of what they don't agree on.
- *Forcing someone to accept or overpowering* someone is not good practice unless it is the only remaining option to ensure a successful audit.
- *Compromising* assumes that everyone can accept less than they originally asked for, resulting in no one getting exactly what they wanted.
- *Collaboration or problem solving* seeks to find a mutually agreeable solution to the conflict—a "win–win" scenario.

Collaboration is always the preferred method of handling conflict but must sometimes take a back seat to the realities of ensuring a successful audit. There will be times when the lead auditor has to listen to input from both sides of a disagreement and just "make the call."

REPORTING

Reporting of supplier audit results is fairly standard across industries and goes something like the following:

- *Quality management.* Every audit report
- *Supply chain management (and/or procurement).* Every audit report
- *Supplier.* Their audit report
- *Site management.* Supplier audit results summary report
- *Site management.* Supplier audit program evaluation report

Audit report distribution of risk-based quality audits, however, is a bit different because such audits and their results are more high profile. Due to the fact that risk management can address public safety and environmental protection, as well as business viability, there is much higher visibility at the director or vice president level for risk-based supplier audit reports. In fact, depending on the nature of the findings, the lead auditor would, in some cases, escalate report distribution to top management even when they wouldn't be on the normal report routing. A typical individual supplier audit report will include:

- Audit purpose and scope
- Audit criteria
- Lead auditor and audit team members
- Summary of results
- Result details, including identified risks
- Audit finding definitions and explanations
- Review of findings (nonconformities, opportunities for improvement, and positive practices)
- Review of corrective actions
- Identification of the need (or not) for a follow-up audit
- Opportunities to improve for *your* organization

The risk-based individual supplier audit report will also address:

- Identified supplier risks and their assessments
- Risk mitigations
- Residual risks
- Any risks attached to how *your* organization conducts business with the supplier

A summary of supplier audit results, along with an assessment of supplier audit program effectiveness, should be presented during the formal management review required by ISO quality management system standards. This should also include, at times as indicated by organizational procedure, those organizations whose quality management systems are ISO conforming. For those organizations who are not ISO certified and who do not claim conformity, the summary of supplier audit results and supplier audit program assessment should be delivered to top management as directed solely by organizational procedure. Following are typical topics that would be addressed within the supplier audit results summary report:

- Summary statement of conclusions based on the data presented
- Any assumptions made in drawing conclusions
- Trending and coding
- Any risks identified by trending of data that should be addressed
- Results of any mitigations put in place based on the previous meeting
- Assessment of the supplier audit program against previously established performance metrics
- Review of findings over time
- Review of causes

The summary of supplier audit results should then be used as an input for both the continual improvement and risk management processes by upper management.

CLOSURE

The expectations for audit closure are also based on risk. Generally, audit closure occurs upon reaching one of four conditions:

- Upon distribution of report (only when no nonconformities)
- Upon acceptable response to report and proof of implementation of accepted corrective action
- Upon presentation of evidence of successful effectiveness verification of the corrective action identified in the accepted response (best practice)
- Upon successful conclusion of a follow-up audit (when due to the number or severity of nonconformities, risk dictates that a follow-up audit is required)

AUDITING "HACKS"

- Once you have developed a checklist, or other audit working papers, that works well and gives you good results, turn it into a template. This will serve as a reminder of what to review when next auditing the related area or function. This will promote greater consistency between audits and auditors. It will also establish a minimum bar for what is to be accomplished during a particular audit. I say "minimum bar" because it is important not to let templates and preprepared checklists handcuff you as an auditor. Each audit is different, and we as auditors should always look to see how we can improve on the practice of previous audits. Thus, while a valuable tool, established templates and "canned" checklists should be the beginning of audit preparation, not the end result.

- This "hack" is related to the first one. When you have a well thought-out audit form, type in the information while you are conducting the audit. This may slow you down somewhat, however, the closing meeting report-out will be much easier because you won't have to comb though pages of notes in order to identify and list your findings in an easy-to-present manner. Also, we know that our other duties will likely start pulling at us as soon as we return to our home sites. This often distracts from or detracts from the time needed for the final steps necessary to complete, submit for review, and distribute the audit report. By typing as much information into the form as possible while on-site at the supplier, you will find that the time needed to generate and distribute the audit report once you return to your home site will often be more than cut in half
- If auditing is your profession, begin to build your own library of standards. It is incredibly convenient to have files that you can easily refer to on your own computer when you wish clarification on specific requirements. Most companies have a subscription to those ISO standards that are relevant to them, which employees can access. Download them to your work computer. If you leave one company to go to another, check the standards library of your new employer first thing for what standards there are that you need to add to your new work computer. Sometimes, when attending a paid training you will be given a copy of a standard as part of the materials. In that case, you can take that copy of the standard with you if you leave one job for another. As in many other professions, so it is with auditing—knowledge is power.
- Don't be afraid to share or collaborate. I wrote an article that was published in *Quality Progress* providing a framework for objectively and consistently evaluating an internal audit program. I created the form in MS Word. One reader asked if he could

have permission to use the form, to which I replied "certainly, as long as you retain my copyright on the documents." The gentleman agreed and sent me a copy of the modified form that he had created for his organization's use based on my original template. He had converted my original Word file into an Excel spreadsheet with cells containing calculations, a second tab for notes, and a third for graphs, resulting in a format that both functioned better and was more visually appealing. He graciously allowed me to adopt his new and improved version for my own use. So by sharing and collaborating I arrived at an even more valuable tool to aid in the continuous improvement of my own audit program.

DESK AUDITS

A desk audit, also known as a *document audit*, is a review of an organization's documents by an auditor. It is one of the first audit steps taken to ensure that an adequate quality management system is maintained. It is referred to as a desk audit because it can be conducted at the auditor's desk since there is no requirement to walk the manufacturing floor or interview auditee employees. One benefit of a desk audit is that it guides the lead auditor in where to focus limited resources when conducting the on-site portion of the audit. It also provides information that helps in the preparation of more-detailed checklists and questionnaires. Another benefit of desk audits is that if it is determined during this documentation review that an adequate quality management system is not maintained, the audit can be terminated at that point and requests for corrective action may be submitted as appropriate. In such a case, conducting the desk audit would save the cost of travel for an on-site audit that would not have been successful. As we have just discussed, a desk audit can be conducted during the planning phase of an on-site audit. A desk audit can also be a stand-alone audit if risk indicates that, while an assessment of the quality management system is needed, the expense of an on-site audit is not warranted.

The key to successful desk audits is to request sufficient documentation to effectively assess the auditee's quality management system and to schedule adequate time for that review. Reviewing just the quality manual doesn't get it. There is not enough detail at that level of documentation. Following is a partial listing of some of the documents that might be requested as part of a desk audit:

- Quality manual

- Contract review
- Control of nonconforming material
- Corrective and preventive action
- Internal audits
- Receiving, in-process, and final inspection
- Customer property
- Complaint handling
- Customer returns
- Customer notification
- Identification and traceability
- Record retention
- Process monitoring and control
- Control of suppliers

Assessment of the quality management system during a desk audit is accomplished by review of the quality manual along with second-tier documents (for example, standard operating procedures) against external requirements (such as regulations and ISO standards) and against internal requirements (like quality agreements, purchase orders, and product specifications). Third-tier (work instructions, drawings, flowcharts, and so forth) and fourth-tier (records, forms, templates, and so on) documented information would typically be reviewed while on-site. Some of the things that an auditor is looking to verify during a desk audit are:

- All of the required documents are in place. If so, is all required information contained within?
- Required records are maintained; actual record review would be accomplished on-site (in some cases relevant records might be reviewed as part of a stand-alone desk audit).
- Related documents support and not contradict one another.
- Documents are clear and unambiguous.
- The supplier ISO and/or other relevant certifications are current.

- Identification of procedural gaps in meeting expectations of the auditing body or the application of standard practices to common processes (opportunities for improvement).

Something to be wary of is that there can sometimes be a tendency to make desk audits a "check-box" exercise if it is decided that there will not be an accompanying on-site audit. This is a big mistake! A properly conducted desk audit can take hours to complete—minimally between four and eight hours. It is not something to be scheduled to "knock out" over the course of a couple hours during one afternoon. A benefit of desk audits is that other work can be done while conducting the audit. With that being said, a desk audit could take place across several days or even a couple of weeks depending on how busy the auditor is. Thus, it is important to keep track of the audit status to ensure that audit completion doesn't fall through the cracks.

VIRTUAL AUDITS

Virtual audits are closer to on-site audits than desk audits in that they include real-time engagement with the auditee as documents and records are reviewed, such as using video or teleconferencing technology, as opposed to being face to face. Desk audits, on the other hand, are a combination of discrete actions as documents and records are requested and then reviewed off-line by the auditor. Then the auditor contacts the auditee with any questions to be answered and awaits a response. During the desk audit there is a lot of stop, go, and wait as the involved parties conduct the audit asynchronously. Just as a person can get a lot more information and be much clearer in a phone call than via e-mail, there is a similar advantage to virtual auditing over desk auditing. Another significant advantage is that with virtual auditing the auditor can witness and process nonverbal cues, which will help in their interpretation of audit findings. As with on-site audits, a desk audit might be a *part* of a virtual audit, as the auditor might want to review certain documents ahead of time in order to optimize the time spent "live" with the auditee. There is a risk in conducting virtual audits in lieu of on-site audits in that certain nonverbal cues may be missed and the auditor may draw incorrect conclusions. So, the benefits of performing virtual audits must be balanced against the risks.

Videoconferencing can range from using the Skype for Business application on your computer to having a $100,000 videoconferencing center with multiple workstations, 72-inch monitors, and deluxe swivel seating. There are also many free and low-cost applications that allow for video-conferencing if budget is a significant issue. In a pinch, you could even use Apple's FaceTime if you had to. The key is that there has to be a matching system on each end of the conversation. The boundaries of real-time engagement through virtual auditing are only limited by the technology available to all parties. At one company, I witnessed a 13-inch monitor on a radio-controlled wheeled platform projecting the face of a manager that could speak with individuals in the area. The platform contained a camera that could see activities going on within the office and on the manufacturing floor. This happened to be within one facility, but imagine if you could use similar technology across sites or between companies! Both desk and virtual audits go through the same reporting and closure process as on-site audits.

CASE IN POINT

We May Have Become a Little Complacent: Or a Practical Application of Risk-Based Thinking

For an example of how to apply risk-based thinking to an audit, let's look at the following true scenario. Company ABC has a supplier XYZ just outside of San Francisco that has successfully produced a part for 20 years. At various times, they have outperformed competing suppliers. Per new supply chain guidelines, supplier XYZ was included on the year's audit schedule since they had never been audited previously. Everyone assumed that, based on past performance, the audit would go swimmingly. That's why I included them on *my* audit schedule. Alas, such was not to be the case.

As part of my preparation for conducting the audit, I made copies of the documentation packets for the last three shipments received prior to the audit date. It was my intent to perform a backward trace as part of the audit. The first step—after I had arrived, introduced myself, and been through the site tour—was to ask to see their documentation for the last three lots shipped. As expected, what they had in their files matched what I had in my hand. Check. Based on the fact that this was such a small shop, I began thinking to myself, "Hmmm, maybe I will even have time to stop by the wine country on my way out of town." Next, I asked to see the production records for the three lots in question, to which the auditee representative responded, "You have the records." I responded, "Are you saying that you sent the milling, inspection, test, and other production records along with your certificates of conformance and analysis?" "Oh no, we didn't do that. Let me get you the production records." What they brought back was a six-by-six-inch square box jammed full of slips of paper. This didn't *seem* like a lot of production records, but I wasn't sure how they segmented their records and wasn't exactly sure what I was looking at. This wasn't an immediate concern since their production records were documented on six-by-nine-inch sheets of paper. So I asked, "Are the production records that I am looking for in this box?" "Well, no." This reminded me of a comedic sketch that I watched once where the comedian was getting frustrated because his partner didn't understand what he was asking and began saying to the "straight man," "*Do you understand the words that are coming out of my mouth*?"

At this point, I began to speak a little more slowly and loudly (as if this would help) as I repeated myself. What I would like to see . . . are the milling . . . inspection . . . test . . . and other production records . . . for these . . . three . . . lots. Pause. "Let me get the owner."

Owner: "So you want to see the production records for these three lots?"

LBC: "Yes, I do."

Owner: "You see we have been making these parts for a long time."

LBC: "Yes, you have. Almost 20 years."

Owner: "These kinds of records can take up a lot of space over the years."

LBC: "Yes, they might."

Owner: "Well, we may have become a little complacent over the years."

LBC: "Please tell me more."

Owner: "We decided last year to only keep the production records for the previous month's runs. We only keep the shipping certifications and other documents for longer than that."

LBC: "Okay. Well, what would happen if we notified you of a problem with a lot that you shipped more than a month ago and asked you to investigate what happened?"

Owner: "We wouldn't be able to."

> LBC: "Well, you can see where I might be concerned with this practice, can you not?"
>
> Owner: "Yes, of course. We have been producing these parts for so long that we have become complacent and made a bad decision."
>
> LBC: "Thank you for your frankness in explaining your process. We will revisit this finding during the closing meeting."
>
> Owner: "Of course."

Next, I went into the metrology department and saw this really cool $10,000–plus laser micrometer! (I know, my inner geek is showing.) It was used to measure the diameter of the blank rods that would be milled and processed to eventually become our parts. While the area supervisor was demonstrating how to use the device, I noticed that the calibration sticker on the side said 2009. Did I mention that this audit took place in 2014? I'm now thinking, "Maybe I won't get to the wine country after all." When I inquired as to why the calibration sticker said 2009, the supervisor replied that they had it calibrated after the initial purchase in 2009. I then asked, "How do you protect from drift and ensure that the laser micrometer remains accurate after all of these years?" "Well, we check it daily across the full range of values using gage pins." Since this is an acceptable practice, I asked to see the gage block set that was used to calibrate the laser micrometer. He showed me, and I found the set to be completely well maintained and in a padded wooden box made to house the pins. However, when I flipped the box over and looked at every exterior and interior side, I had to ask, "Where is the calibration sticker for the gage pin set?" "Oh, those aren't calibrated." Starting to speak slowly, *again,* "Okay. So how do you know that these gage pins are accurate?" "We check them with the laser micrometer." (This time I paused . . . .)

My response: "Well, whatever standard that you use to calibrate a piece of equipment that is used to accept product has to be calibrated by a standard having traceability back to NIST (National Institute for Standards and Technology). So, you can use the gage pins to calibrate your laser micrometer as you have described, but those gage pins must themselves be calibrated." Pause. "Let me go get the owner."

When all was said and done, there were two nonconformities concerning calibration, one for the quality manual, and one for records maintenance (or lack thereof) raised during the audit. If this were a new supplier assessment, the supplier would have been rejected out of hand. However, Supplier XYZ has consistently had one of the best quality and on-time-delivery records. Now what to do? Apply risk-based thinking to the situation!

It is at this time when proper assessment of the level and type of risk is important. Because none of the nonconformities directly impacted product or product realization, and based on both recent and past history, the risk to product was deemed low. However, the risk to successful implementation of the QMS (the ability to monitor the effectiveness and efficiency of the company quality management system and determine root cause when something goes wrong) was high. In other words, despite Supplier XYZ's excellent historical production record, if something did go wrong in the future, the supplier's ability to detect and respond effectively could be negatively impacted by these findings.

All four findings were classified as major, and Supplier XYZ was downgraded from "approved" to "conditionally approved" status on the approved supplier list. From the perspective of Company ABC, orders could still be placed with XYZ as long as the findings were responded to with effective corrective action within a six-month window. So, other than a loss of face, no business harm would come to Supplier XYZ as long as they determined and implemented a robust corrective action plan. Also, rather than schedule the next audit for three years ahead, as would typically be the case, it was determined that a follow-up audit should be conducted the following year. These measures allowed Company ABC to take a firm stand in order to address future risk while still acknowledging the solid performance history of XYZ. Supplier XYZ did implement corrective actions as promised and passed a follow-up audit.

CASE IN POINT

Catfight: A Tale Showing the Pros and Woes of Virtual Auditing

By Shauna Wilson

> *Nonverbal communication between people is communication through sending and receiving wordless clues. It includes the use of visual cues, such as body language (kinesics), distance (proxemics), and physical environments/appearance of voice (paralanguage), and of touch (haptics). It is estimated up to 65 percent of communication is nonverbal; it has been said, "The most important thing in communication is to hear what isn't being said."*
>
> —Peter F. Drucker

Late one evening in an online meeting with a client in another part of the world, I was provided feedback on a recent internal audit conducted virtually. My findings included three different responses to a shared process. As I met virtually with three gentlemen who sat together in a conference room, I reported my findings to them using a collaborative program to illustrate the objective evidence. We used no cameras, thus, we could not see one another. English is my first language, but it wasn't theirs. I explained my findings and asked a simple question—which process is correct? There was a long silence, and then suddenly an argument broke out. Exacerbated by the sound of a different language and the speed with which they were spewing their words, from my end it sounded like a catfight. As they argued, I thought, "Would they have behaved this way if I was there in the conference room or if we had cameras on?" As suddenly as the argument started, it stopped. All was quiet! Breaking the silence, I asked them for their decision, and the manager responded in English with the process to be used.

> *An eAudit is a systematic, independent, and documented process to obtain evidence through electronic means to determine the extent of conformity to the audit criteria.*
>
> —J.P. Russell

In this story an interstate and international internal audit conducted virtually found process failures and communication issues between entities located in three countries. An advantage eAuditing offers over face-to-face (FtF) auditing is the ability to conduct a whole system review of the global supply chain with the same auditor connecting the distal processes together. This finding might have been missed if conducted in a traditional FtF audit with limited locational boundaries and multiple local auditors. An eAudit or virtual audit uses the same audit process as an FtF audit except for conducting the audit through electronic means at remote locations. Unlike a desk audit, eAudits are simultaneous, where the auditor and the auditee are present in their remote locations, viewing documents or processes simultaneously over collaborative programs. Virtual teams have communicated and worked together online for 20 years, but the use of auditing virtually or eAuditing is still not an accepted audit method by most registrars. Many report that European registrars will not accept internal audits that are conducted virtually. Stated validation concerns include the ease of hiding things from auditors and limited nonverbal communication. Admittedly, the auditor conducting eAudits will need more skills in technology and communication methods, and knowledge of cultural differences, to be successful.

For instance, auditors need to understand communication methods, including how to replace nonverbal communication and mediate self-monitoring behavior. Nonverbal communication includes facial expressions and body language often used in FtF communication. Self-monitoring behavior is focused on changes in an individual's behavior when not meeting FtF. Self-monitoring behavior is rated in terms of high or low behavior. Simply put, people with low self-monitoring behavior do not self-govern their behavior when they are not physically present; behavior can include tardiness, rude comments, and reading e-mails or texting during a virtual meeting. High self-monitoring people do not have to be watched; they are able to keep the same standards of politeness and respect in both FtF and virtual environments.

Reliance on nonverbal communication is a primary method of communication in most cultures. The lack of nonverbal communication can be a barrier at times when cameras are limited. Audible nonverbal cues, like voice tone changes or a delayed response, can become an indicator to ask more questions on a subject. But, in this story, it was not the nonverbal communication that exposed miscommunication between the entities. It was preparation and skillful auditing, asking thoughtful questions, and following audit trails and objective evidence that discovered the process failure. In a way, eAuditing may move auditors to depend less on nonverbal communication and focus more on the audit and communication processes and research methods to find objective evidence. Cameras may help to manage low self-monitoring behavior but will not completely replace all aspects of FtF nonverbal communication. In the story, would cameras have prevented the outburst or been forgotten like the microphone, which could have been muted during their conversation?

The argument was the result of a miscommunication; either we did not communicate that correctly, or the communication was taken out of context and misinterpreted. Communication is blamed for most things that go wrong in our personal and business lives. Yet, most people are unaware of communication processes that will help others to understand information. A communication process commonly used for laying the groundwork for a conversation is the three-stage communication development approach. The initial stage focuses on *background research* on a subject matter, person, or event. For example, many people instantly Google or ask friends about topics before going to an interview. The second stage is a *discussion* phase with the person after the initial research, where people will talk about commonalities to build trust. An important aspect of the second stage is the decision to make collaborative plans and continue to stage three. People can decide not to continue to stage three if they are not committed to work toward the same goal. In stage three, people *jointly lay a path to work together*, those in new relationships will meet regularly, and teams begin new processes. In audits the three-stage communication approach can be applied to the audit process, as shown in Figure 2.9.

In preparing for the audit's closing meeting, I used the three-stage communication model to outline communication steps and address potential variables related to nonverbal communication, self-monitoring behavior aspects, and technology. Table 2.1 outlines the stages associating related variables.

I had assumed a miscommunication issue between all parties as the root cause. What I did not understand was the foundational process that needed to be followed. During initial research (stage one), I met with senior management, with whom I shared my finding and from whom I received information regarding the foundational standard process. The manager's feedback gave me information clarifying why the processes were not aligning. Learning these details, the closing meeting (stage two) needed to illustrate to the three members the objective evidence and its overall result of divergent processes. To remove blame, the results had to be clear and visual in order to impart an understanding to mitigate any low self-monitoring behavior. Because of the distance over which the party met together, I decided that respectfulness should stay within cultural norms, even with their culturally competitive nature. In the end, the team members worked together to follow the foundational process. Culture plays a very big role in global supply chain audits. I believe the response was mostly cultural; low self-monitoring behavior may have resulted in someone leaving the meeting or stating agreement without follow-through.

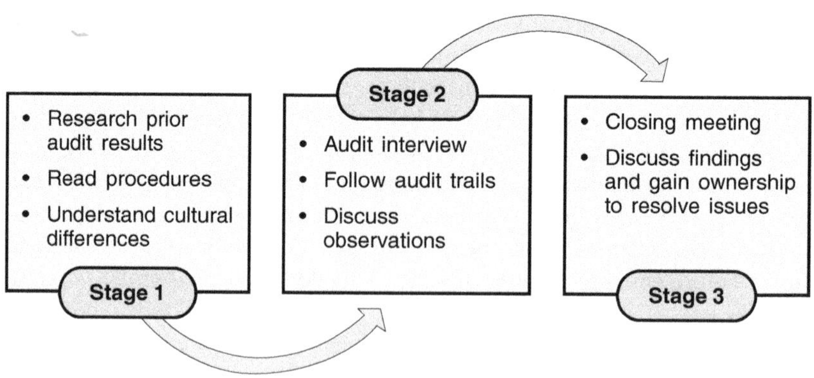

Figure 2.9 Three-stage communication development process.

An overlooked aid to eAudits may be the newly released ISO 9001:2015 standard and the requirement to understand the context of the organization. The new standard leads us to understand just how complex businesses have

Table 2.1 Three-stage communications model.

Three-stage communication development stages	**Potential communication variables**	
	Nonverbal communication	**Self-modification behavior**
Stage 1 Passive social information-seeking prior to speaking to others; assess working environment and gather background information	Understand: • Nonverbal communication indicators within a cultural sense • No cameras or visual appearance for the auditor – Only audio • Auditees are meeting FtF, the auditor is remote	Seek knowledge on cultural differences: • The response to feedback or critique • Competitive work environment • Competitive culture
Stage 2 People discuss experience, find commonality, and share process issues	Replace nonverbal communication with: • Clear display of the audit findings • Clear statement of discovered process gaps • Remove the personal and location reference	Prepare for: • Auditees meeting FtF; self-monitoring behavior at remote site should be high; face saving should be active • Response will be cultural and the nature of the work environment highly competitive
Stage 3 People decide to either make plans or not become involved in the solution	• The discussion at the remote location gave an impression they were fighting. It was unintelligible due to language differences, but the reaction is considered cultural	• No one left the room • Each team member committed to improvement plans and followed through to resolve issues

become by competing in a global market. When the context of the business is understood and interested parties are identified, risk-based thinking tools could include a hybrid auditing model for understanding quality system performance. A hybrid auditing model may include multiple methods like eAudits, FtF and desk audits, supplier reviews or regular yield reporting, random third-party product testing, and customer surveillance audits (auditors posing as customers).

eAuditing in a hybrid model is an efficient and effective audit method optimizing the use of limited resources. The following activities can leverage eAuditing methods:

- Visual verification at an external provider's location to understand process-related issues
- Reviewing product-related issues in real time at a remote location, or verifying that a change has been implemented
- Enhancing understanding among interested parties because everyone can see document content or processes simultaneously

Companies that invest in eAuditing allow remote locations to learn from one another as they gain a better understanding of remote processes, and leverage and standardize common processes. Rather than refusing eAuditing methods, prioritize to invest in the technology training. Practicing online facilitation, learning new skills to replace nonverbal communication, and engaging in intercultural studies should be at the forefront of both internal and external auditors' professional goals.

Shauna Wilson, *President at Amazon Consulting Inc., is a performance management consultant designing efficient and effective quality systems. Shauna is an IRCA-certified auditor and leading expert in remote auditing. She holds an MS in performance management technologies/instructional design. Shauna wrote* InterneTeaming.com: Tools to Create High Performance Remote Teams *and coauthored* eAuditing Fundamentals: Virtual Communication and Remote Auditing, *and was featured in* Quality Progress, The Auditor, *and ASTD's* InfoLine. *Shauna is the Education/Social Responsibility Chair at 607 Portland ASQ Section and currently serves as the USTAG Expert for PC/TAG302 ISO19011 Auditing Management Systems.*

Chapter 3
International Auditing

So, you have been assigned your first international audit. You are excited, maybe a little nervous, and wonder how it might be different from the many domestic audits that you have done. As with any audit, thorough planning is key to success, though with international audits it is even more crucial. First of all, you should add 30 or more days to the typical lead times that you build into your domestic audit planning for the following reasons.

TRAVEL LOGISTICS

Getting a Reasonably Priced Fare. The lowest fares sell out farther in advance for international than domestic flights. Most employers allow an upgrade to business class for flights longer than a certain duration. These seats are also limited.

Getting a Reasonable Flight Plan. I only had to have a trip go from 24 hours to 36 hours because the tickets were purchased too late (still three-plus weeks in advance, though) to find a reasonably priced fare one time to make me vow that would never happen again. International layovers can be 18 or 20 hours or more if you are unlucky (unless that layover is in a great city, then that is another matter entirely!). If you are stuck in an airport for an extended period of time, consider taking advantage of the wonderful lounges that many have. You can often shower, rest in comfortable lounge chairs, or get reasonably priced meals for one nominal fee.

Getting Your Preferred Seat. I am only five feet, eight inches tall and can fit in most places, but I imagine that being six foot or taller and sitting in a middle seat for 10 or more hours is *not fun*! Also, if you have a broader stature or any physical conditions where you would prefer one seat over another, it is most important to get your desired seat when on an eight-hour or longer flight. Getting your preferred seat is more likely the earlier that you book.

Acquiring Needed Passports or Visas for Team Members. Passports and visas can take from four (if you pay "rush" fees) to 10 weeks to acquire, depending on the country you are traveling to. You don't want to purchase international plane tickets for audit team members and then not have their passport or visa arrive in time. Some countries may delay okaying a visa if the passport is too "old," for example, expiring within three months of the travel date. Obtaining visas could also become an issue if anyone on your team has any "unacceptable" items in their background.

Clearances. Those individuals requiring clearances for their primary jobs must be careful of which countries they travel to, and confirm that none of the suppliers on their audit list are in countries on the "no travel" list for people with clearances.

Currency. Be sure to have some currency with you because many businesses where you might want to shop abroad may not take credit cards. It is best to have local currency with you, although most places will take U.S. dollars. You don't want to broadcast that you are from the U.S. in certain parts of the world. Consider getting local currency from an ATM. Often, their exchange rates are cheaper than the international currency exchange booths at the airport.

Meals. Meals on international flights are free and fairly tasty, often providing regional fare as one of your options. When in the airport during layovers, find your gate before stopping to eat. You may assume that gate 42a is just a short distance from gate 39, but depending on the airport, that may not be the case. You don't want to be in a situation where you are short on time and the gate is much farther away than you thought. Also, include in your planning how you will meet any dietary restrictions you may have while traveling, and allow for the possibility that when traveling internationally, the auditee may require greater advance notice to accommodate your dietary restrictions or possibly may not be able to accommodate them at all.

Security. Know where the U.S. Embassy is and how to contact them should you require assistance. Be especially careful when traveling to countries where there are elements that are not friendly toward the United States.

- Use RFID protective wallets to prevent your personal information from being scanned right off of your credit cards by the latest malicious technology.

- Be careful not to flash cash or otherwise broadcast that you are carrying currency.
- Keep your passport with you at all times.
- Be clear on how you are to identify your contact and who they should be.
- Ask your contact if there are any additional security precautions that you should take.

AUDIT PLANNING

Allow for time to translate documents (if desired) when auditee documents and records are not written in English. Although you can hire a professional translation service, getting auditee documents translated does not have to be expensive. You can see if you have anyone that reads the auditee's language that works for your employer, or use a program like Google Translate to give you enough of a translation that you can begin to create your checklists. It should be noted, however, that when you use Google translate specifically, you are potentially placing proprietary documents on a public forum. So, I would use Google Translate and similar open-source free translation tools with care.

Translation. Do you want to hire a translator, have someone on the team that can translate, or allow the auditee to provide translators? (Most manufacturers in developed countries around the world have at least one and probably several members of management that speak English—often they have studied in U.S. universities.) It is also important to note that for the Romance (Spanish, Italian, French) and Germanic (for example, German and Dutch) languages, you can often make out enough of the meaning of a document to generally understand what it is saying, and you will only have to ask questions about the specifics. When this is the case, it is helpful because you can then stretch your translation resources further.

Audit Strategy. Because it is easier to understand something when it is being described while you are looking at it, you may want to spend a greater proportion of your time than usual out on the floor when the native language of your auditee isn't English. Since you will only have limited, if any, ability to read and understand the documents for yourself, witnessing activities taking place may help you better understand the processes that you are there to audit. Also, as a general best practice, it is better to trust what you see than what you read.

In the States, one person from the auditee staff often is assigned to each auditor in order to facilitate acquiring requested documented information as quickly as possible. For international audits this may not be possible as you might only have one person on staff who is available that knows English well enough to support the audit. This means that you will have to plan in advance how one audit team member will be able to continue to audit while another is being helped by the escort. The key here is to avoid one or more auditors sitting and doing nothing until the auditee escort can help them.

International Travel. This can be both expensive and time-consuming, so obtaining a reputable regional third-party contract auditing service is a choice that some companies make. Once a company decides that it will conduct its own international audits, it is important to try to arrange to audit more than one auditee while in the region if at all possible. Often, coordinating dates with two or more auditees can add to the planning time for your audit.

Multiple studies have shown that as humans, we can subconsciously be prone to *confirmation bias*. Humans don't like to change their opinions once they have been formulated; rethinking our beliefs once they are formed can be both difficult and uncomfortable. These studies give substance to the old adage that you "only have one chance to make a first impression." This truth is especially important in business where, for certain cultures, social considerations can be as important as business factors in developing business relationships. Research the culture(s) that you will encounter during your trip to minimize the likelihood of unintended offense. Understand local business etiquette as best you can. Who you greet first when you enter a room, how you proffer your business card, how you sit, even how you gesture, can all unintentionally cause offense. And let me tell you, until you have been told not to gesture with your index finger or show the soles of your shoes, you don't realize how often you cross your legs when sitting or gesture with your index finger! In Muslim countries, women need to dress conservatively and be more "covered up" than they might be in other countries given the climate or time of year. Consider learning how to say, "hello," "thank you," "you're welcome," and "goodbye" in the local language. Understand that in some cultures it would be an insult to refuse a gift (within limits of course). Also in some cultures, while not expected, bringing a small gift representative of your homeland would be considered appropriate and appreciated. Some good sources (free and paid) for information on cultures around the world can be found at https://www.cia.gov/library/publications/the-world-factbook/, www.infoplease.com, and http://online.culturegrams.com/.

OTHER CONSIDERATIONS

Plan any additional logistics caused by team members arriving at the destination from different points in the United States or arriving at different times.

If you have to catch a connecting flight after clearing customs, you should allow yourself at least an hour and a half between flights so that you are not stressed and rushed in trying to make your connection. Some international airports have multiple security checkpoints, which could also delay transit from one flight to the next.

Be careful not to over- or under-pack. Plan out the clothing that you will need (business and casual) for each day. Leave room in your suitcase for gifts and souvenirs.

Wow. Planning for an international audit is not as simple as you thought, huh? If you think that this is a lot to remember, let's look at what happens once you arrive in a foreign land.

To begin, if at all possible, you want to arrive two days before your audit is scheduled to start. This way your body can begin to adjust to the time difference; plus, it gives you an additional day to recover after what will be a long and tiring journey. Confirm with the auditee that you have arrived safely in town (assuming they weren't the ones to pick you up from the airport). Also, be sure to have at least one contact phone number from the auditee who you can call after hours if any issues arise that you cannot handle. As you arrive in town and throughout your visit, you will want to take into account any local safety concerns above and beyond the standard security precautions you employ when traveling domestically. Robbery, fraud, kidnapping, identity theft, and more can occur at or near airports or expensive hotels, and in seemingly ideal settings. For example, in Shanghai on Nanjing Road (their Fifth Avenue), ATMs are in booths built into building walls with doors in order to prevent distance viewing and theft of your credit card number and PIN. At a $300-a-night hotel in downtown Cape Town, your room key is checked by security before you are allowed to go up on the elevator to your floor. You need to research not just the culture, but also any potential safety or security risks in the area that you are traveling to. During your last audit team meeting before beginning the audit on the next day, you will go over audit purpose, scope, and assignments, as well as any potential work-arounds expected from conducting an audit at a non–English speaking facility. Additionally, you will want to go over any cultural basics that you feel would be important for getting off on the right foot—do you greet the highest-ranking person in the room first, proper exchange of business cards, any nuances regarding male–female interaction, and so forth.

When auditing here in the United States, we often use a combination of the element and process approaches. The ratio of the methods used (50/50, 60/40, and so forth) would be determined by the purpose of the audit, the nature of the auditee, and a variety of other factors. When auditing a facility where you don't speak the predominant language, you should plan to spend more time out on the floor than typical. Walk the process. Let the process approach take prominence. It is easier to understand something when you are looking directly at an activity taking place. Allow longer time for the facility tour—90 to 120 minutes (to allow for stopping, asking detailed questions, and taking notes) instead of the typical 30-minute tour that we would expect here in the States. You would still want to use the element approach, as well as matching the auditee's internal procedures and records to external requirements. Here's how.

In the States, it is easy to be spoiled when conducting audits. We usually have more than one person pulling documents and records to support the audit, and there is often one person per audit team member! When traveling internationally, you will have, at times, one person who speaks English that you have to share among your audit team members. When this is the case, it is important to implement a strategy that will allow for other team members to continue working while one auditor at a time engages with the interpreter. Auditors can and should try to understand to some extent the context of documents presented in one of the Romance or Germanic languages until it is "their turn" with the interpreter. Typically, there are enough clues to confirm the thrust of a required document. Make notes for specific, more-detailed questions to ask when the interpreter becomes available. Thus, the time needed with an interpreter when reviewing documents or records is minimized. Look at the following list of the French, Spanish, German, and Italian words for "segregate" and "nonconforming" to understand how this could be the case:

- French: séparer, non conforme
- Spanish: segregar, no conforme
- German: trennen, nicht konform
- Italian: segregare, non conforme

When you are working with the interpreter, it is especially helpful to use tiered questioning:

- Please explain how your so-and-so process works.
- Where does it say that in your procedure?

- What is your evidence that this process is implemented as described?

As you are managing time for your audit, you will need to factor in that going through the interpretation process will make everything take longer. Also be aware that, even when translated into English, some words may have a different meaning across different countries. For example, I have found that the concept of *process variation* can mean different things at different companies in different countries. You cannot assume that the supplier understands what is meant or intended even when they nod their head in response. Definitions must be specific, and complete understanding of what is being said should be confirmed. Review process maps and flowcharts, when available, to understand how work flows throughout the facility, and help identify areas of possible concern.

Consider the example below of questions you might ask to assess the "control of nonconforming material" process in a facility that you are auditing where the number of English speakers is limited. You will notice that in addition to asking for explanations, you ask them to "show me" how they implement their system. Also, to "show me" in documents and records evidence of what they have described. Again remember, at least in the Romance languages, you can often more or less make out what is being said if you know what you are looking for. In non-Romantic languages, look for completed records, though you then will have to take the auditee at their word.

- What do you do when nonconforming material is found?
- How do you document nonconforming material?
- How do you disposition nonconforming material?
- How do you identify the material itself as nonconforming?
- How do you keep nonconforming material from being used?
- Is what you have told me documented in a nonconforming material procedure?
- Can you show me where in the procedure?
- Can you take me to examples of nonconforming material in your facility so that I can verify that it is segregated and/or marked as you describe?

Finally, and most importantly, the vast majority of suppliers, both foreign and domestic, want to show off their facility, want to provide quality products, and want to support a successful audit. With proper planning and strategic implementation of auditing best practices, while taking into account cultural and language differences as well as logistical obstacles, we can help them to do so.

CASE IN POINT

The Congolese Bienvenue: When Audit Logistics Are Unusually Difficult

By James Metto

One of my worst experiences as an auditor occurred when I used to work with an international certification body that was in charge of clients in the East and Central Africa region, with the regional office based in Nairobi, Kenya.

The scope of the certification services included carrying out ISO 9001 and ISO 22000 audits for one of our clients in the Democratic Republic of the Congo (DRC). DRC is one of the countries that we covered in our certification activities. The DRC borders the Central African Republic (CAR) and South Sudan to the north; Uganda, Rwanda, Burundi, and Tanzania to the east; Zambia and Angola to the south; the Republic of the Congo to the west; and the Atlantic Ocean to the southwest. It is the second-largest country in Africa by area and eleventh largest in the world (https://www.britannica.com/place/Democratic-Republic-of-the-Congo).

The client had operations in several regions of this expansive country. The audit planning needed to be seamless considering the distance to be traveled within the shortest time possible in order to reduce the number of man-days that would be spent on non-audit activities, such as travel. Taking into consideration the geography of the audit sites, a whole month was dedicated to auditing this particular client at its head office in Kinshasa as well as the regional sites.

In the audit cycle of the year 2007, we scheduled to audit this client during the months of August and September. The audit planning was carried out as usual, and upon confirmation by the client, a team of two auditors embarked on the audit process starting in the last week of August.

The audit process during the first two weeks was concluded successfully with no incidents. Things took a turn for the worse, however, on Sunday, September 9, 2007. We began our day normally in Kinshasa, DRC, but at around 1100 hours local time we decided to step out of the guest house to buy a few necessities. As soon as we set foot out of the gate, a maroon Mercedes-Benz pulled up beside us. One of the guys in the front of the vehicle showed something like an ID badge identifying himself and his three colleagues as police officers. They then proceeded to inquire if we were army officers, to which we responded in the negative. They then demanded to see our identification papers. We complied, expecting this to be a normal routine check by the security officers. The questioning, however, was anything but objective, and it became clear to us in a short while that their intentions were not good.

Although we had the correct visas on our passports, the guys then claimed that the visas were tourist visas and not work visas; hence, they concluded that we had entered DRC on the wrong visa, which they claimed was a criminal offense. Without any warning, we were forcefully shoved into the car and sandwiched in the back seat, with the guys purporting to take us to the police station to be booked for entering the country illegally, as well as for further interrogations.

As soon as we entered the car and the vehicle started moving, the guys on each side started searching us on the pretext of looking for guns. Finding none, they grabbed our wallets, which they handed over to the guy in front, who seemed to be their team leader. This fellow cursed us, mentioning something to the effect that we were lucky to be Kenyans, otherwise, he said, had we been Rwandese or Ugandans, we could be dead in a short while. During this period, there was a war that had sucked in several neighboring countries, including Rwanda and Uganda. This was the genesis of the anti-Rwanda and -Uganda sentiments from this fellow since the two countries were considered to be supporting antigovernment rebels during the war.

As part of the intimidation, one guy pulled his gun and held it in the direction of my colleague's head. They demanded to know if we had given them all our valuables and searched us again. My colleague hesitated when surrendering his valuables, and this caused him to be further harassed. One of the fellows got hold of his private parts and asked, "What's this? A gun?" My colleague, finding it odd, had to respond to make the guy remove his hands and said, "It's my thing." This became our inside joke in the office. I would occasionally ask him, "What's this?" and he would answer like he did while we were held hostage by those characters: "It's my thing."

They drove us in circles for a period of about 30 minutes around the quiet suburbs of Kinshasa. Then all of a sudden, the team leader spoke something in French, knowing that we did not understand. Almost immediately, the driver stopped, got out and moved to the back of the vehicle, which we discovered later was to cover the vehicle identification plate. At this point, we feared for the worst. We saw hostilities that clearly demonstrated that either these fellows were rogue police officers or outright crooks pretending to be police officers. When the driver returned to his driving position, the leader handed back our passports and wallets, but, of course, without the money. They demanded that we get out of the car with the speed of light, or else we would be past tense. Without wasting a second, we got out of the car as fast as our feet could carry us.

Once we were out, they sped off, leaving us in a secluded area with little or no traffic. Traumatized and confused by the episode, we went in the opposite direction of the vehicle. While walking, we kept wondering how the audit, scheduled to take place the next day, was going to happen, not to mention how we would communicate with the client, having lost our cell phones to the thugs.

After we walked some ways, we noticed a building named "[Something] Justice." We prayed that we might get some help there, if not justice. Lost in a foreign land where language was a barrier, someone came our way who must have been a godsend and, to make it even better, knew English. After relating the incident, the guy confirmed that such episodes had been on the rise, especially with foreign nationals. Our spirits were lifted even more when the stranger showed a lot of concern and helped us back to our guest house by paying the taxi/bus fee. We kept wondering what would have happened had we encountered another group of thugs; we probably would not have lived to tell the story.

Although we were happy that we finally reached the guest house, another problem awaited us. We needed to catch a flight within the next hour to the eastern part of the country for the next audit. But we did not have our client contacts and mobile phones. Luck, however, seemed to be on our side that day. Although the guest house assistant had little understanding of either English or Swahili, a language spoken in East Africa and parts of Central Africa, we somehow made him understand that we needed help from the client contact person. He managed to find someone who could relay the message to our contact person. Our logistics contact person was then able to speak with us, and we explained our dilemma. Fortunately, he was not far away from our location, and he managed to come and facilitate our airport transfer. We just made it, thanks to a flight delay, to our next audit destination.

The last two weeks of the audit at the remaining sites were subdued compared to this initial experience. We managed to conclude the audits successfully thanks to encouragement and moral support from the client. Upon returning to Nairobi, my colleague could not imagine that he might have to go back for another audit in the DRC in the near future, so he resigned to join a different organization. I, however, continued to carry out system audits on behalf of my organization for another three years before deciding to move on to new challenges. Indeed, the experience was a true Congolese "bienvenue" (welcome) that will forever be a marker in our audit experience.

James Metto *has a Master of Science degree in environmental legislation and management, as well as a Bachelor of Science in agricultural engineering. He has extensive experience in quality and environmental management system auditing in engineering, manufacturing, chemical, and service industries, covering first-, second-, and third-party audits. He is an ISO 9001, ISO 14001, OHSAS 18001, and ISO 50001 lead auditor.*

CASE IN POINT

International Audit Logistics: A Funny Thing Happened on the Way Down the Audit Trail

By Kristen Wagner

My first international audit experience came during a trip to Indonesia to visit my company's sister facility as well as three suppliers located in China. I did some minor research on what to expect from an international travel and audit standpoint, but overall I depended largely on my fellow coworkers' experience and advice. Armed with what I thought were the essentials—enough Starbucks VIA packets to provide coffee to a large army, as well as some medication prescribed to me by my doctor should I get sick—I happily boarded the plane and nestled into my business class napping pod, overflowing with the excitement of seeing two new countries and having my first real international auditing experience.

After two layovers, the plane finally landed in Indonesia. My coworker and I were among the first off the plane. Our prepaid express visa service agent greeted us and promptly asked us to hand over $25 for our visas. I handed him my credit card, and he quickly shook his head and stated without hesitation, "Cash only." The words swirled around in my head—of the five people I had talked to, all five said not to bring any cash and that a credit card would be fine, even after I mentioned that all websites said you should bring some cash. Starting to panic about how I was going to get $25, and what I would do if I couldn't even enter the country, my coworker, who also did not bring cash, hesitantly headed over to the nearest ATM. He used his debit card to withdraw enough cash for both of us to get our visas. The rest of the Indonesian leg of the trip, thankfully, went extremely well.

In China my lack of cash was not so detrimental as I was traveling with three different coworkers for this leg of the audit, all of whom only brought cash. Unfortunately, the second full day in China I became extremely sick. Without going into major detail, I spent the night burrowed in the hotel bathrobe emerging only to commit an act that I thought would surely leave me for dead every 30 minutes. If I had to have chosen between cash and the medication from my doctor, I was thankful I brought the medication.

The third day was reserved for auditing the second supplier. Equipped with backup clothes in my briefcase should the worst happen, I entered their cleanroom manufacturing facility and was instantaneously confused. The supplier's survey had boasted of their cleanroom environment, including cleanroom shoes worn throughout the entire facility. What I saw upon entering were Hello Kitty, Big Bird, unicorns, cats, and dogs, all in the form of large, fluffy, squishy slippers. These were the cleanroom shoes the supplier had praised in their survey? I watched with curiosity as a woman walked past me, the bells adorning her slippers jingling, and the fake fur on each foot gently rustling against the other with each step. I scanned the feet of all the employees in every room we entered and met eyes with hard black plastic ones of various cartoon characters and animals—all more grandiose than those that I had seen in the previous room.

Finally, it was the end of my trip, and I was set to fly back after two weeks of being abroad. I headed toward the international counter at the airport and was promptly sent back to the domestic area. It was a complete surprise for me—I was unaware my layover to Beijing counted as domestic, even though, looking back, it makes complete sense. I headed toward the check-in agents and soon realized they hardly spoke any English. We tried (and failed) to communicate the best way we could in English and with what felt like an interpretative dance about where my luggage was going to go. With time no longer in my favor, I just nodded "yes" in understanding and hoped that I wouldn't lose my luggage.

Because our interpretative dancing went on longer than expected, I barely boarded my plane in time. I entered the plane, and both flight attendants stopped in their tracks and stared at me, and for good reason. I was a young white woman—alone, breathless, and near tears from overexhaustion and stress—entering a plane filled with nothing but Asian businessmen in suits. They stared at me a bit longer, unmoving, before I managed to utter, "Do you speak English?" in severely broken Chinese. They both shook their head. One took my ticket and pointed to my seat in business class—I was the only one there. I paid no attention to the safety talk since it was all in Chinese. Once you hear one safety talk, you have heard them all, right?

Once we landed, a very small Asian woman in a kimono-style dress entered the plane, walked up to me and stated, "Follow." That was it. I hesitated for a moment before I grabbed my items and walked down the stairs to the tarmac. She stated, "Follow," again as she opened the door to a golden-colored minivan. At this point, I had no idea where I was going, didn't really care anymore, and just wanted to be home. Once the minivan stopped, she exited the vehicle and then stated, "Follow," again. I followed her down a corridor lit with flickering lights and smelling of musk. It was just her and me. After about 10 minutes of walking and me starting to assume I was never going to make it back to America, we finally walked through a wooden door and entered a very large, but completely deserted, room with three luggage belts. She then stated, "Bags here," then left as quickly as she had come. I awkwardly stood in the room by myself for what felt like an eternity, wondering if I had misunderstood something. I obsessively checked my watch every few minutes, fearful that I was going to miss my flight. Finally, people flowed into the room and the belts started to move. I spotted my luggage, grabbed it off the belt, and proved it was mine to the agent by the security door. A few hours later I found myself in a business class napping pod once again, finding complete solace in having my own language and knowing that I would be back in my own bed in less than 30 hours.

Overall, I would not change a single aspect of the audit or the trip. I learned a great deal, both with respect to international travel and about auditing:

1. I should have been more proactive in preparing for my trip beyond what my coworkers had advised me to do and the brief research I performed.

2. I should have brought cash, against the advice of others (and a small package of toilet paper would have helped in some places as well—don't ask!).

3. I should have had a small book with more local language phrases with me as Google Translate (which I had actually used to converse with a band in Indonesia quite successfully) promptly stopped working once I entered China.

4. I should have walked step-by-step through my itinerary with my travel agent and asked more questions.

5. What suppliers put in surveys is not always exactly true. Did my supplier lie about cleanroom shoes? Not exactly. It is always important to confirm written facts with witnessed facts. That is why it can be helpful to bring a copy of the initial supplier survey with you when auditing a supplier for the first time.

6. Unexpectedly, not hearing my native language for such a long time was very hard. Yes, there were interpreters, but interacting with someone who speaks your language as their first language is very different. This was actually quite eye-opening for me,

experiencing it firsthand as opposed to just "trying to understand" what others feel like. It has definitely made me more sensitive to those who are in a country where their native language is not predominantly spoken, and has made me more willing to openly stand up for those who are being mistreated because of it.

7. On a lighter note, I will *always* bring that miracle medication my doctor prescribed for me when traveling abroad. Also, the coffee throughout the entire trip was actually amazing—no VIA was needed!

Kristen Wagner *is a Senior Supplier Quality Engineer at Vision Ease, a recognized leading manufacturer of quality ophthalmic lenses, where she manages the supplier audit program. Kristen has a BS in materials science and engineering from the University of Minnesota. Over the past three years, Kristen has worked on implementing supplier development best practices, including reenergizing a supplier assessment program, helping drive improvement, and mitigating organizational risk as a result of these efforts. She is responsible for supplier auditor training in addition to serving as lead auditor for both domestic and international supplier audits.*

Part II

Supporting Skills

Chapter 4

Auditor Soft Skills and Ethical Considerations

The secret of man's success resides in his insight into the moods of people, and his tact in dealing with them.

—J. G. Holland

Mastering technology is no longer enough to ensure continued business success. Mastering various audit tools and methods is no longer enough to ensure a successful audit. In an increasingly international environment, quality and other professional staff must master soft skills that allow them to successfully engage with other employees, clients, and suppliers from different countries and cultures.

The key to mastering soft skills is being a good communicator, being able to work successfully alone or within a team, and working in an ethical manner while understanding the importance of capturing lessons learned beyond the scope of your initial mission.

Three rules for effective communication (from you to someone else) are:

1. *Ensure that the message is clear.* Whether preparing to deliver a speech or send an e-mail you should always ask yourself *before* the message is delivered, "What am I trying to accomplish?" Are you asking for information? Permission? Are you trying to provide information? Once you ask this question, review your message, whether e-mail or presentation notes, to make sure that it is clear what you want the recipient to do once they have received it.

2. *Verify that the message is received and understood.* Don't assume that because someone is sitting in the room while you are delivering your message that they understand or are even listening to what you are saying. It is important to prompt your audience by asking for some response or feedback to what you are saying. In a one-on-one, consider asking the other person to repeat back in their own words what you said. Do not accept a "read receipt" as acknowledgment that a message is received and understood when the communication is important. All a read receipt means is that the e-mail was opened. Managers in a large corporation can receive up to 300 e-mails a day or more. Yours may not have been fully understood or even read. Ask for some kind of response from the recipient acknowledging receipt of the e-mail and when you might hear back from them in detail.

3. *Utilize the appropriate medium for transmittal.* Often, individuals have preferred methods in how they communicate. For me, it's e-mail; for my wife, it's by phone. You will sometimes start to notice that when you e-mail someone, they always call back, or when you call, they either stop by your office or make arrangements to meet. In the former case, phone is probably the preferred medium of communication, and in the latter, face-to-face communication. Why is this important? When time is of the essence, if you know someone is more responsive to phone conversations, it is best to communicate via phone. Generally, face-to-face conversations are always better when discussing complex issues. Communications that will become part of a permanent record should not be conducted via text.

The great enemy of communication, we find, is the illusion of it.

—William H. Whyte

Effective communication also means avoiding the use of "junk words." Junk words are words (and phrases) that do not add value (information) to the sentence that they are in. They require interpretation from the reader and may lead different readers to draw different conclusions about the same event. One example of junk language is, "I didn't buy the widget because it cost *too much.*" How much is too much? Do we really know? It would be much better and more accurate to say, "The price of $79 was more than I wanted to spend on the widget." Another simple example would be the commonly used phrase "as soon as possible." How soon is that? Two different people could easily respond within two different time frames, one of which may not be soon enough for the requester. As a person who grew up in New York City, and then lived 20 years in the Southeastern United States, let me tell you that I *know* from experience that ASAP can have two totally different meanings depending on where you are from! Use of junk words can rob the message recipient of information that they need to make an informed decision. In the first case, would the widget be too expensive for them to purchase if they wanted it? In the latter, how soon do I need to provide information or assistance?

KEY THOUGHT

How well we communicate can make or break an audit. It can fracture or cement relationships.

So, remember to be language specific when you communicate. Don't use slang, abbreviations, or colloquialisms even when that language is common in your industry. Also, don't forget when on the receiving end of communications that 55 percent of communication is done through body language, 30 percent through vocalization (tone, inflection, speed, volume, and so forth), and just seven percent through words (what we actually say). What does this tell us as auditors? That we need to watch nonverbal communication with our eyes while listening for verbal cues beyond what someone is actually saying to attain the most comprehensive information that is conveyed. This is important because our brain receives information from our five senses according to the approximate percentages shown in Table 4.1.

Table 4.1 Percentage of information received by our brains through the five senses.

Sense	Percentage
Sight	83%
Hearing	11%
Smell	3.5%
Touch	1.5%
Taste	1.0%

A few common "tells" to look for during face-to-face interactions with people are:

- Jaw tightening—tension
- Furrowed brow (frown)—disagreement, resentment, anger
- Eye squinting—dislike, anger, objection
- Leaning/turning away from during discussion—disinterest or disagreement
- Head nod—positive messages, signal to continue (but not always agreement)
- Avoiding eye contact—you and your message are no longer important, deception
- Lip biting, increased eye blinking, sweating, changing behavior—nervousness

It is important to understand, though, that these tells aren't absolute guarantees that you will understand someone's behavior. They are all affected by an individual's baseline behavior, cultural norms, or current situation. So, if all of these factors can impact the importance of tells and the information that they may convey, why bother? Well, reading tells is an important *part* of the total information that we collect, process, and interpret as auditors. Tells are based on general observations and can be very useful, but you still must remember that every person is an individual. Some people may blink more rapidly or sweat more profusely when excited than others, which could throw off your analysis of their behavior. That is why it is important to try to capture baseline behaviors when you can. This is obviously easier to do when analyzing the behavior of a coworker or boss than when meeting someone for the first time during a second- or third-party audit. Cultural differences are equally important. What is assertive in one culture may be seen as insulting in another. What is considered suspicious behavior in one culture would only be considered polite in others. There may also be extenuating circumstances beyond the audit that may lead to an auditee appearing tense or nervous—illness, personal concerns, and so forth.

A tell by itself may not mean much but, when taken into account along with other factors, it may provide important insight. The individual tell is not as important as changes in behavior or speech patterns. Is the interviewee speaking faster, slower, louder, or with more hesitation? What has changed? Is it the topic? Has someone else entered the area? By being in tune to these types of changes in the interviewee, the auditor can possibly identify areas that need further investigation.

Successful auditors must be able to lead a team as well as work on their own. For the lead auditor, it is important to understand that there are different phases in the team-building process, and for each of those phases the role of the leader changes. The four phases of team building are:

1. *Forming.* Coming together, meeting for the first time, understanding the mission.
2. *Storming.* Everyone trying to define their own role within the team, deciding on which approaches to take, assigning tasks.
3. *Norming.* Consensus has been arrived at and working protocols have been established, work is getting done, the project is moving forward.
4. *Performing.* Performance is optimized, everyone understands their role on the team, work is getting done both effectively and efficiently.

The role of the leader in each phase is:

1. *Forming.* Welcoming and providing direction
2. *Storming.* "Selling the vision" and building consensus
3. *Norming.* Cooperation and participation
4. *Performing.* Facilitation

In teams, as with any group of individuals coming together, there can be conflict. Sometimes, the conflict is between the audit team and the auditee, or sometimes within the team itself. Regardless of from whence the conflicts spring, the lead auditor must resolve them quickly and effectively. Some typical methods for handling conflict are:

- *Avoiding* an issue or person is not an option if the conflict is relevant to the audit.

- *Smoothing over* may be an option if the issue is minor or irresolvable. Those in conflict should focus on what they agree on instead of what they don't agree on.
- *Forcing someone to accept or overpowering someone* is not good practice unless it is the only remaining option to ensure a successful audit.
- *Compromising* assumes that everyone can accept less than they originally asked for, which results in no one getting exactly what they wanted.
- *Collaboration or problem solving* seeks to find a mutually agreeable solution to the conflict. A "win–win" scenario.

Collaboration is always the preferred method of handling conflict, but it must sometimes take a back seat to the realities of ensuring a successful audit. Compromise or overruling will sometimes be the method that carries the day.

Time management is also a crucial skill to master, whether you are working alone or with a team. The team leader must:

- Ensure that all planned activities are completed when possible.
- Make allowances when unplanned changes occur.
- Sometimes divert resources when further investigation is needed in a specific area.
- Provide that a thorough audit is conducted even when changes must be made to the audit plan.
- Be cognizant of the auditee's time and availability of staff.

KEY THOUGHT

Auditors must always remember that they are guests of the auditee. As such, they are bound by auditee rules while in the area, and should not touch, review, or copy anything or speak with anyone without first asking permission.

If you don't stand for something, you can fall for anything . . .

—Reverend Peter Ray Johnson

ANSI/ISO/ASQ QE19011S identifies five principles of auditing that are "prerequisites for providing audit conclusions that are relevant for enabling auditors working independently from one another to reach similar conclusions." In other words, two auditors shouldn't audit the same area one week apart and get drastically different results. Each audit takes a sample of data during a different "slice in time," so you wouldn't expect the exact same results between the two audits. The results should be comparable, though, if both the auditors are well trained and utilizing best practices in conducting the audit. While "ethical conduct" is singled out as its own line item, there are elements of ethical and moral behavior in each of the other principles as well:

- Ethical conduct
- Fair presentation
- Due professional care
- Independence
- Evidence-based approach

I have my own ethical credo that I follow, as summarized in these seven tenets:

1. Immediately report any unsafe, illegal, or unethical activities.
2. Do not engage in any unsafe, illegal, or unethical activities.
3. Avoid even the appearance of impropriety.
4. Don't audit an area outside your realm of expertise.
5. Don't audit an area for which you are responsible.
6. Be honest and fair in your dealings.
7. Strive to advance the profession as well as your own knowledge and skills.

Ethics are so important to the auditing profession that you cannot receive an ASQ certification without first reading and agreeing to abide by their Code of Ethics. Also, many companies will have auditors read, understand, and sign a code of ethics as part of their training prior to auditing.

KEY THOUGHT

It is more important to develop your own moral code that you live and work by than to memorize someone else's code that you can cite "chapter and verse" but don't follow.

CASE IN POINT

Differing Point of View

The tale below is true, and the language is as close as memory can provide. The company names have been replaced with supplier WeMakeWidgets (WMW) and customer GHW (GottaHaveWidgets). If you are experienced in audits, you have heard, and probably participated in, some version of the "verbal dance" that follows.

> GHW Customer Auditor: *GHW considers this a partnership that we want both parties to benefit from. We are not looking to find fault. By conducting this audit, we just want to identify ways that you can improve and, also, ways that we can improve. If there is something that GHW can do differently to make things easier for you, I want to hear that as well while I am here.*
>
> WMW Supplier Response: *WMW regards GHW as not just a valued customer but a partner as well. We are always pleased to have a fresh set of eyes to review our systems and procedures so that we can continually improve, and look forward to receiving your feedback.*

It went downhill from there.

After a brief facility tour, the audit started with previous audit results and moved into customer complaints. The conversation went something like the following.

> GHW: . . . *It states in our quality agreement that GHW complaints will be communicated from our quality department*

to yours. Sometimes, though, complaints also come in from our purchasing and project management departments and may be transmitted to your quality department or sometimes to your customer service department.

WMW: *The quality agreement does state that complaints should be transmitted from your quality department to ours. However a complaint comes in from GHW, though, we ensure that it is logged in within 24 hours by our quality department, and responses are communicated within the required time frame per our procedures.*

GHW: *Yes, I see that. Your responses are timely, your investigations thorough, and your corrective actions are robust. However, it states in our quality agreement that GHW complaints will be communicated from our quality department to yours. I will have to discuss this with our team when I get back. For now, though, we can move on.*

Imagine WMW's surprise when, during the closing meeting, it was indicated that a nonconformity would be written against them for not processing complaints from GHW's quality department to theirs! But the problem originated with GHW! What was WMW to do? Refuse complaints that weren't received from the GHW quality department? The auditor acknowledged that while the problem originated within GHW, WMW was still technically in violation of the quality agreement by acting on complaints received from GHW departments other than quality.

Little did the auditor realize that this unyielding and unreasonable interpretation of the facts annihilated any possibility of an open and transparent relationship between GHW and WMW. After all, if WMW could be written up for something that the auditor acknowledged was caused by GHW, then how much worse might it be if there was a question on the part of WMW, or the need for clarity on some ambiguous area of the contract or quality agreement? Better for WMW to figure things out for themselves and then establish a "defensive position" if the decisions made become an issue. Thus, chances for future information sharing and collaboration were greatly hindered because the auditor representing GHW was viewed as unyielding and draconian in their interpretation of facts, and, by extension, GHW as a company was now perceived as being that way.

To add insult to injury, two days after the auditor left, WMW Company received a customer complaint from the GHW *purchasing* department! To his credit, the WMW quality manager responded to their purchasing manager and copied the auditor's manager that they couldn't respond because they had just been written up by the GHW auditor for responding to complaints that were not communicated from the GHW quality department to the WMW quality department, and to please advise on how to proceed. By using humor (and just a bit of sarcasm) the quality manager was able to drive home his point. The ridiculousness of the finding was acknowledged and overturned, but the damage to the relationship between the two companies had already been done.

CASE IN POINT

Managing a Difficult and Nontransparent Auditee: The Power of Subliminal Messaging

By Janet Bautista-Smith

As a Logistics/3PL provider, most of the customers we encounter are from different company cultures and have one shared element. That element is the pressure of getting freight delivered intact and in a timely manner since there is a very narrow window for error in this competitive environment. This narrative focuses on delivery issues caused by customer error rather than the Logistics/3PL company. The root causes and data audit analysis performed by the Logistics/3PL company involved a rather intricate path, as shown in Figure 4.1. The action required to correct the problem was an easy fix, but the journey of extracting the root cause during the data audit performed by the Logistics/3PL company, who was originally blamed for the error, is the point of this narrative.

The customer's manager in charge of the supplier specification was very defensive upon learning the results of the root cause analysis performed by the Logistics/3PL company (pointing to the manager's error) as shown in Figure 4.1. During meetings, this manager resorted to intimidation, using colorful curse words and making unprofessional statements such as "You, Transportation Manager—you are stupid, so stop talking."

To make a long story short, the logistics quality director attended one of these meetings and used a "subliminal message strategy" to stop this concerning behavior displayed by the manager. At the beginning of the meeting, the quality director requested permission to record the conference call for note-taking purposes. As expected, this manager objected to the

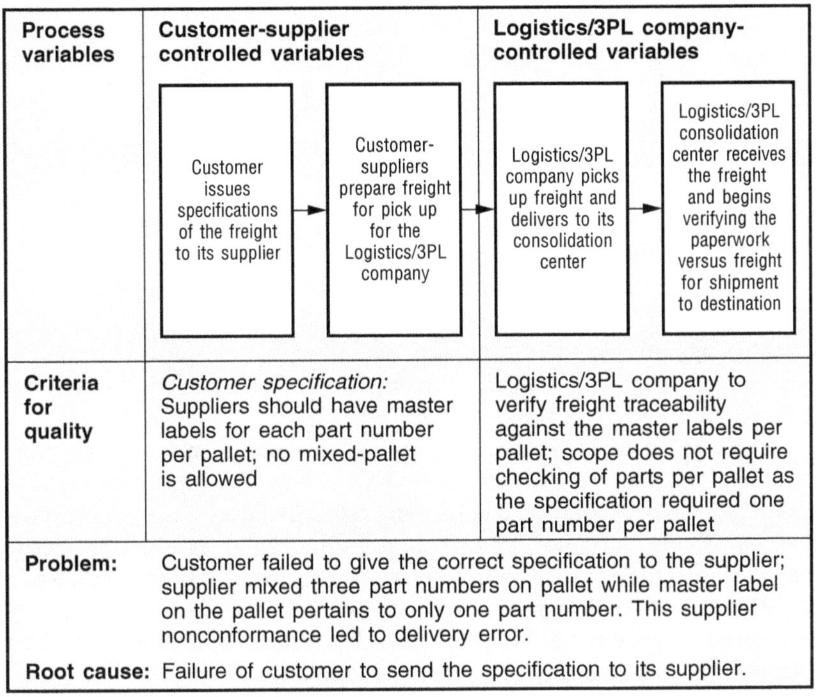

Figure 4.1 Root cause analysis diagram.

conference call recording; however, he uttered no curse words during the meeting.

Lesson learned: a change can occur without actually "fighting the war"; sometimes, a strong subliminal message can be just as effective as outright confrontation, or even more so.

Janet Bautista-Smith *is the author of two ASQ-published books,* Auditing Beyond Compliance *and* The Art of Integrating Strategic Planning, Process Metrics, Risk Mitigation, and Auditing. *She is the director of quality assurance and continuous improvement for ProTrans. Janet has a BS in chemical engineering and holds the following ASQ certifications: Six Sigma Black Belt, Quality Auditor, Quality Engineer, and Manager of Quality/ Organizational Excellence.*

CASE IN POINT

You Can't Judge a Book by Its Cover

By Sheronda Jeffries

What do you do when not only your conclusions are challenged, but your credentials and your ability to lead an audit?

I started working as a third-party auditor conducting ISO 9001 audits with a large certification body a little more than two years after graduating from college. At that time, I was short, and I looked younger than I actually was. I was much younger than most of the other auditors, but I was also a full-time auditor. I was auditing a *lot.*

An audit team had been assembled to audit a large, multisite organization that had once been recognized for its innovation and quality. However, due to numerous leadership changes and other challenges, the organization was now struggling simply to meet the requirements of ISO 9001. Not only had leaders come and gone, but staff turnover was at an all-time high, while organizational morale was at an all-time low.

I was assigned to audit the organization's calibration activities, and let's just say that the results were not pretty. Actually, the results were pretty dismal. It seemed as if no one had explained the concept of measurement traceability to the staff. When I attempted to trace back to the calibration standard used on specific equipment, to establish a relationship to internationally or nationally recognized standards, it was nearly impossible. While reviewing the audit findings with the team after completing my audit interviews, I tried to explain basic metrology concepts to the calibration technicians, and they politely listened. I could see, though, that they either didn't believe me or had no clue as to what I was trying to say. Finally, I told them that based on my audit results, I would recommend to the team leader that the calibration findings be classified as a major nonconformity, which could impact their certification. Again, either they didn't believe me or they didn't understand, although I tried my best to explain.

At the daily wrap-up that evening, after discussing my findings with the audit team and audit team leader, I presented my audit findings to the auditee organization. Of course, the calibration technicians were in attendance. I shared my audit findings and explained the impact of the major nonconformity on the organization's certification. When the lead technician saw the seriousness of everyone in the room, he began to understand the severity of the audit findings and the jeopardy they placed on the organization's certification. At this point, the lead technician became visibly angry. He shouted out, "How can you trust that what she said is right? She is just a kid. Why couldn't the audit team leader audit our team?"

I remained calm and did not immediately respond. I didn't have to. In response to the lead technician's outburst, the audit team leader replied, "That 'kid' trained me to audit, so everything that I learned about auditing, I learned from her. She could have led this audit team."

After the daily wrap-up, the other calibration technicians thanked me for taking the time to review and discuss my audit findings. Although they were disappointed in the results, they commended me for my thoroughness and professionalism.

The moral of the story is don't let anyone judge you by your age or appearance; remain calm and professional and show them that what's important is how well the job gets done.

Sheronda Jeffries *is a program manager for Cisco Systems where she provides consulting and training. She has 20-plus years experience as a third-party auditor and as a consultant to Fortune 500 companies. Her experience spans information and communication technologies (ICT), testing laboratories, and electrical, mechanical, paper, and plastic manufacturing. Sheronda is also an industry leader representing Cisco Systems at QuEST Forum, an industry collaboration of companies dedicated to ICT quality and performance. She represents QuEST at the USTAG TC 176 and USTAG PC 302, ISO TC 176, ISO CASCO STAR, and the IAF, where she serves as users and industry director.*

Chapter 5
The Twenty-Five Questions

Philosophical Yin and Yang

A thoroughly planned project is already 80% successful.
No plan survives first contact with the enemy.

By any means necessary.
The end doesn't always justify the means.

Look before you leap.
Fortune favors the bold.

The above paired statements all present sage advice, yet all seem diametrically opposed to each other. The difference is context. There is rarely a "truth" or "wisdom" that is perfect for every situation. A decision must sometimes be made "in the moment" as to what is the best choice to make. That is often the case when conducting audits. Such decisions are assisted by the questions that you ask. There is a narrow path in between the two contradicting sentiments, and the practice of *twenty-five questions* will help guide you to and through it. As auditors, we don't necessarily know (or need to know) how to solve problems. What we need to be able to do is ask the right questions. To ask the obvious ones. To let one question lead us to the next until all of the key questions are asked and you as an auditor can draw a fact-based conclusion. Let's look at an example where we align our questions with the different audit phases—planning, execution, reporting, and closure.

PLANNING

Planning questions should look to the past, present, and future. What does the last audit report, supplier scorecard, public information, and discussions with colleagues tell us about this supplier (history)? What is our strategy based on current goals, available resources, and risks (present)? What resources are needed to successfully conduct the audit (future)?

1. What are we trying to accomplish?
    a. What type of audit will this be?
2. What does a successful audit look like?
3. What are the relevant reference standards?
4. Have we confirmed authority, purpose, and scope?
5. What can be accomplished before arriving on site?
6. What information do we need/have access to?
7. What are the needed resources?
8. What is the approach/strategy?
    a. How will we communicate?
    b. With whom and when will we communicate?
9. What percentage of audit time should be spent in gemba?
10. What will our sampling plan(s) be?

EXECUTION

During the execution phase, questions based on responses are paramount. You have to be able to go where the audit trail leads. This can sometimes be to unexpected places.

1. What are the key processes?
2. What are the key support processes?
3. How do you know when processes are performing well?
    a. Is there clear flow-down from organizational goals and objectives?
4. How well are process interactions understood?
5. How are risks and opportunities managed?
6. How fully does each process reviewed fulfill relevant regulatory/standard requirements?

7. How do we know when to conclude the fieldwork phase of the audit?

REPORTING

During reporting you need to determine whether risk dictates a nonstandard report distribution. For safety, legal, or potentially significant business-level risk, you will want to include a higher level of management on the distribution list.

1. What is our reporting protocol?
   a. What is our report distribution?
   b. What are our timelines for report submittal and response?
2. What is our report format?
3. What attachments should be included with the report?

CLOSURE

For closure, you need to know if risk dictates that a follow-up audit will be necessary. Are there any CAPAs related to the audit, and if so, what is the relationship between closing the audit and closing the CAPAs?

1. What are our closure conditions?
2. Have we met the criteria for closure based on audit results?
3. What is the closure process?
   a. Will a follow-up audit be needed?

KEY THOUGHT

You will notice that in this set of questions you have substantially more planning questions than in the other categories. That is because planning is so very important in completing a successful audit. It is a true maxim that a well-planned audit is already more than 50% successful. You will also note that there are 23 questions and not 25. Twenty-five questions *is meant to be a description of the method and not an absolute requirement. You ask the number of questions that you need to get to where you are going.*

When employing the practice of twenty-five questions you will find sometimes that obvious questions are naturally paired. At other times the next obvious questions will be dictated by the auditee's response. Some examples of asking the obvious questions are:

- How do you perform this task?
- How do you *know* how to perform this task?
- What objective evidence can you show me that the procedure you described is being followed?

It is always important to understand how individuals are trained to accomplish specific tasks, what records are kept, and what objective evidence is available. It is also important to understand whether there are different training protocols required due to the complexity or risks of certain tasks.

> Auditor: *How do you perform this task?*
>
> Auditee: *What* I *do is . . .*
>
> Auditor: *Are there other/different ways to perform this task?*

When someone implies that there is more than one acceptable way to perform a task, you should probe further. Is the procedure unclear or not being followed? Are there indeed multiple allowable ways to perform a particular task?

> Auditee: *This is a new/revised process.*
>
> Auditor: *What are the steps in approving this new process/ change for production?*
>
> Auditor: *Do you have objective evidence that your procedures are followed that you can show me?*

When a process is new or has been changed, it is important to understand what the approval process is to "green-light" that process or process change for production. If the process is one that is validated, you will want to ask whether a new full or partial validation is required per their procedures.

Figure 5.1 shows a twenty-five questions template with spaces for questions asked and for the expected objective evidence. If the evidence is other than expected or nonexistent, then you will document those facts in the objective evidence column during the execution phase of the audit.

Twenty-five questions and related objective evidence	
Questions	**Potential objective evidence**
Planning	Planning
1.	1.
2.	2.
3.	3.
4.	4.
5.	5.
6.	6.
7.	7.
8.	8.
9.	9.
10.	10.
Execution	Execution
1.	1.
2.	2.
3.	3.
4.	4.
5.	5.
Reporting	Reporting
1.	1.
2.	2.
3.	3.
4.	4.
5.	5.
Closure	Closure
1.	1.
2.	2.
3.	3.
4.	4.
5.	5.

Figure 5.1 Twenty-five questions matrix.

CASE IN POINT

The Power of the Process Approach: Driving Smarter Questions That Lead to More Meaningful Audit Findings

By Denis Devos

Several years ago I was conducting a registration audit as a certifying body (CB) auditor at a midsized chemical company. Toward the end of the audit, while auditing the shipping process, I was introduced to the young lady who looked after dispatching tanker trucks and releasing loads. She demonstrated for me how she fulfilled an order and dispatched tanker trucks to their customers. Everything was being done in accordance with procedures and it appeared to be a well-managed process. The young lady concluded her demonstration of the shipping process by stating that her very last step was to issue the invoice.

Using process thinking, and knowing that an incorrect invoice could negatively impact customer satisfaction, I asked a simple question: "Do we ever make a mistake on the invoice?" To my surprise, the young lady replied, "Yes, all the time!" Admittedly, the question was not intended to further extend the audit, but was asked almost out of habit. Good process auditors are constantly asking about next steps and connecting dots based on what they know is important to an effectively running organization.

With this unexpected response to my question, now it was time to follow the audit trail. My follow-up question was "Oh, I see . . . how often does that happen?" She responded, "All the time—and I have to keep track of that to make corrections." At this point she reached into her bottom drawer and pulled out a spiral-bound lined notebook. Now, an auditor knows they've really hit pay dirt when they are able to get the auditee to reach into the bottom drawer of their desk. I took the notebook and began to leaf through the pages. There was approximately one page per month, and each page had 30 lines on it. That meant there was an average of one invoicing error every day! As I leafed through the notebook, I made use of a seemingly naïve question to advance the audit. "Wow—this looks like a lot of adjustments . . . what do your customers think of this?" She laughed and said, "Are you kidding? They think we're idiots." Her use of that term suggested to me a high level of customer dissatisfaction, so I continued. I asked her how these mistakes happened, and she explained that regional sales representatives make their own deals to give discounts to their larger customers. These deals are allowed, but the discounts are never communicated to the plant where orders are shipped. Therefore, all the shipping clerk could do was issue an invoice based on the pricing information she had in her computer. When customers complained that they didn't get the deal they were promised, she had to confirm the discounts with the salesperson and issue a credit memo for the difference. She was frustrated with all of the extra time and effort that these adjustments required. Talk about waste!

My final question was "What is your team doing to fix this?" She explained that she had brought the issue to the VP of sales several times but that nothing was being done to address the issue. At this point I told her that earlier in the day I had audited the QA department's corrective action process and that it was among the best I had ever seen (which was actually true). When I asked her if she thought their strong corrective action process in QA could help her, she was enthusiastic. "Can we do that?" I wrote a nonconformance stating that their invoicing process was causing customer complaints that weren't being addressed in their quality management system. When I presented this nonconformance in the closing meeting, I saw the plant manager nodding his head in agreement—he knew that this problem existed and wasn't being addressed by the sales team. As the meeting ended, the plant manager actually thanked us for identifying the issue and told us that our audit report would finally bring action on resolving it.

ISO 9001 does not include requirements for invoicing, but going beyond verifying conformity with specific clauses of the standard, understanding the process approach and the concept of customer focus, opened up an audit trail that resulted in a value-added finding for the organization. A strong focus on the process approach combined with a strong knowledge of an organization's processes can provide the kind of unexpected insight that drives an organization forward.

Denis Devos *is a professional engineer with a long career supporting the automotive industry. He is a Fellow of ASQ and is a recognized expert in the application of the ISO 9001 and AIAG 16949 standards. Denis was the developer of the* Risk Is the Compass *risk-based audit model in 2001. He works with clients in a variety of industries, providing internal audit services and training for QA practitioners and internal auditors. Denis is a regular contributor to ASQ conferences at the Audit Division and Management Division, and the World Conference on Quality and Improvement.*

Chapter 6

A Little Data'll Do Ya: Basic Statistics and Data Analysis for Auditors

So, what is a process approach anyway? Hold on now! This chapter is about data analysis for auditors, isn't it? Well, yes, but before we can talk about how auditors can analyze data, we need to understand the processes from which the data come. Quite simply, a *process* can be thought of as an activity that transforms inputs into outputs. In manufacturing, the 6 M's—man, machine, material, measure, method, and Mother Nature (working environment)—are often identified as process inputs. It is understood that, typically, problems with process outputs come from problems with process inputs. This is the relationship shown in Figure 6.1.

In other words, the root causes of nonconforming outputs tie directly back to the process inputs. You don't always need to use the 6 M's, though. It's only important to identify inputs that make sense for your organizational processes. Data from most process outputs align themselves in a *normal distribution*, or *bell-shaped curve*. The bell-shaped curve is a graphical representation of *process variation*, of which there are two kinds. *Common cause variation* is that which is normal to any process. Trying to eliminate common cause variation will not work and might potentially make things worse. *Special cause variation* is that which is caused by an external factor,

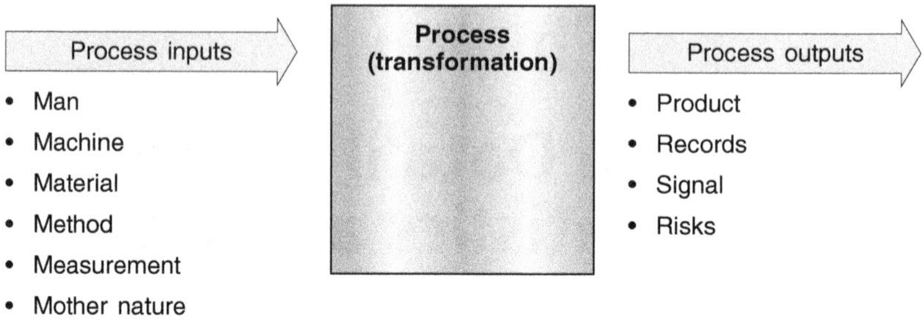

Figure 6.1 Process map.

and should be investigated to determine root cause and then apply corrective action.

Having a normal distribution is important because bell curves allow for a more profound understanding of process behavior through the use of statistical tools and methods, for example, in understanding whether a given process is producing normal variation or if some special cause is adversely affecting it. It can also show whether there is a statistically significant difference between two events, in other words, how likely a specific event is to occur or how likely a value is to fall within a specific range. Let's take a look at the example of an organization that has a delivery service whose on-time delivery (OTD) has dropped, averaging 86 percent OTD over the past three months. They decide to utilize a more expensive delivery service in hopes of receiving a higher OTD rate. For the first three months, the new delivery service has an average rating of 91 percent. Did the organization make a wise decision paying more for the new delivery service? The answer is unknown. The improvement in OTD could be due to natural variations in the process, and the original delivery service might have been expected to experience the same uptick in service rating. Or the improvement in the OTD score may have truly been due to improved service provided by the new company. By using statistical techniques, the organization can arrive at a true and unbiased answer.

Another more-detailed example of the benefits of using statistics to make a fact-based decision is the scenario where company XYZ had increasing sales for a new product line and were trying to decide when to add a second shift, and whether it would be full time or part time. They knew that their sales averaged 96 units per day, and that once they averaged 100 units per day they would need to add a shift. So, they were close, but how close were they? The sales data approximated a normal distribution, so they decided to use a Z-table to help make their decision.

Z-SCORE

The average monthly sales since last February is 96 UPD (units per day), with a standard deviation of 3 UPD. What percentage of the days had sales greater than 100 UPD?

From the Z-table, with

$$\text{Z-score} = \frac{X - X}{\sigma} = \frac{100 - 96}{3} = 1.33$$

we find a value of .4082, which means 40.8% of the population lies between 96 and 100.

We then take 40.8 and subtract it from 50 (50 – 40.8 = 9.2), so 9.2% of the days had sales of 100 UPD or more.

Since they were only hitting 100 units per day less than 10% of the time, it was decided to handle any surges in sales using overtime until sales increased further. Using statistics allowed company XYZ to make a

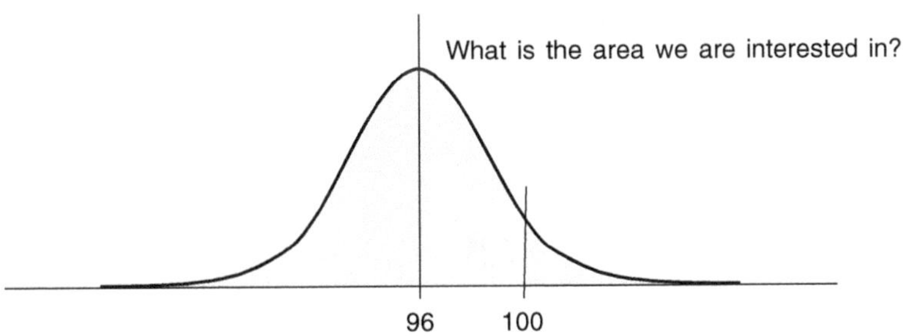

Figure 6.2 Sales frequency distribution.

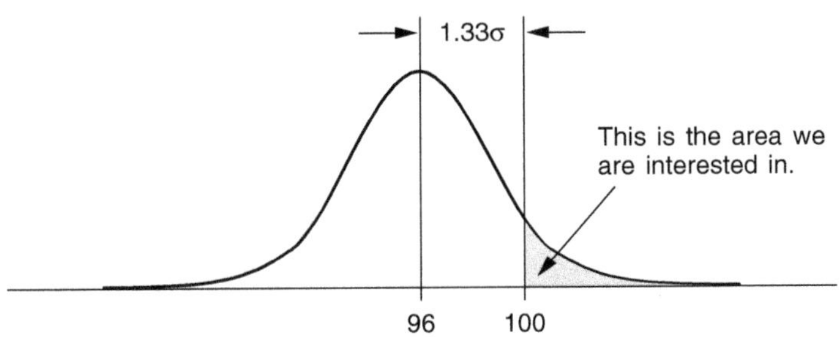

Figure 6.3 Frequency distribution showing percentage sales > 100 UPD.

fact-based decision that they had confidence in as to whether or not to add a second shift at that time.

Note: The Z-table to which the z-score is linked is a table of values showing how likely a value is to fall within a given range based on how distant that value is from the process mean (average) in standard deviations (measure of process dispersion or width).

The benefits of normalized data are so important that when process data don't fall into a normal distribution pattern, the data are often transformed. Transformation is a kind of "statistical hocus-pocus" that seeks to answer the question "What would the data look like if they were normally distributed, and which statistical tools can we apply based on this theoretical model?" Data transformation is, thankfully, outside the scope of this book.

The process width of six standard deviations (± 3 standard deviations from the process center, or mean) is considered the *voice of the process* (VOP). This is the portion underneath the bell-shaped curve where 99.7 percent of the data fall, as shown in Figure 6.4.

Someone way smarter than me decided years ago that 99.7 percent was a high enough percentage of the population from which to draw conclusions about the entire population. It is the ± 3 standard deviations from the process center where control chart control limits are set (Figure 6.5). Variation

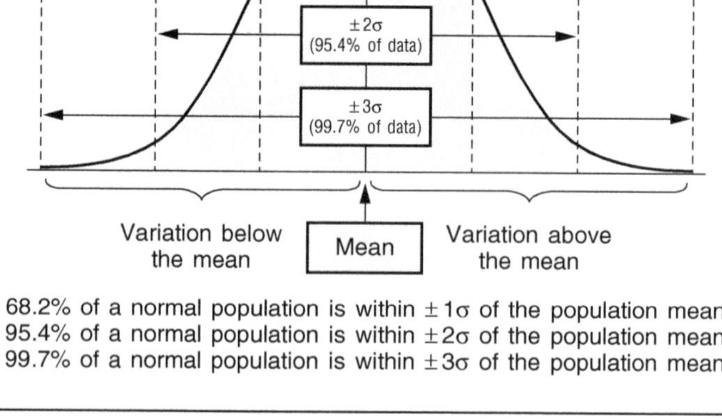

Figure 6.4 Standard deviation and the bell-shaped curve.

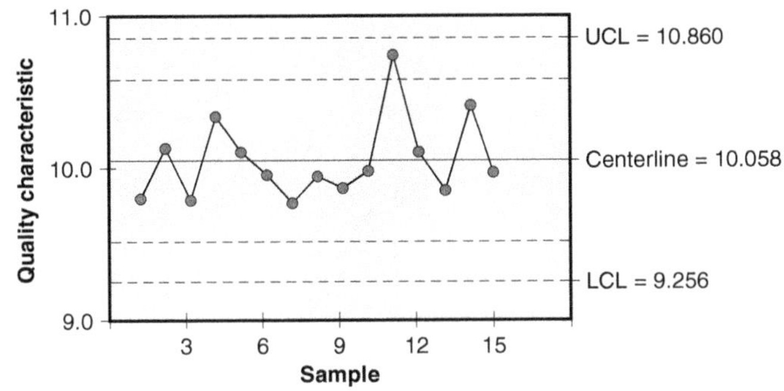

Figure 6.5 Sample control chart.

that causes data points to fall outside of the ± 3 sigma control limits is called *special cause* variation. It is important to note that "uncontrolled" doesn't necessarily mean "out of specification." You want control limits to be within specification limits so that if a control limit is passed, you have time to either troubleshoot the process or make adjustments before parts begin to consistently go out of specification. These are the two most important things to understand about a process: Is it stable and in control? Is it capable?

Process capability is simply the ability of a process to consistently make parts to specification. Process capability indices compare the process width to the difference between the upper specification limit and lower specification limit. The most commonly used capability indices are C_p, C_{pk}, P_p, and P_{pk}. The capability index is 1 when the voice of the process equals the voice of the customer. Less than 1, and the process is not capable. An industry rule of thumb, when a capability requirement is called out in a specification, is having C_p/C_{pk} be greater than or equal to 1.33, and P_p/P_{pk} be greater than or equal to 1.67. This translates into the VOP being approximately 75% of *voice of the customer* (VOC), allowing that the process may shift somewhat over time but will still produce parts within specification.

Comparing the VOP (six standard deviations) to the VOC (upper specification limit – lower specification limit) for each quality characteristic deemed critical derives C_p and P_p, as shown in Figure 6.6. In other words, C_p or P_p = VOC/VOP, where the higher the capability index, the more capable your process. The weakness of C_p and P_p is that these indices do not take into account where the process is centered. That means you could have a very high C_p or P_p, but you could still regularly produce out-of-specification parts if the process mean is shifted too far in either direction from the midpoint between the upper specification and lower specification limits. C_{pk} and P_{pk} rectify this problem by taking into account the distance of the

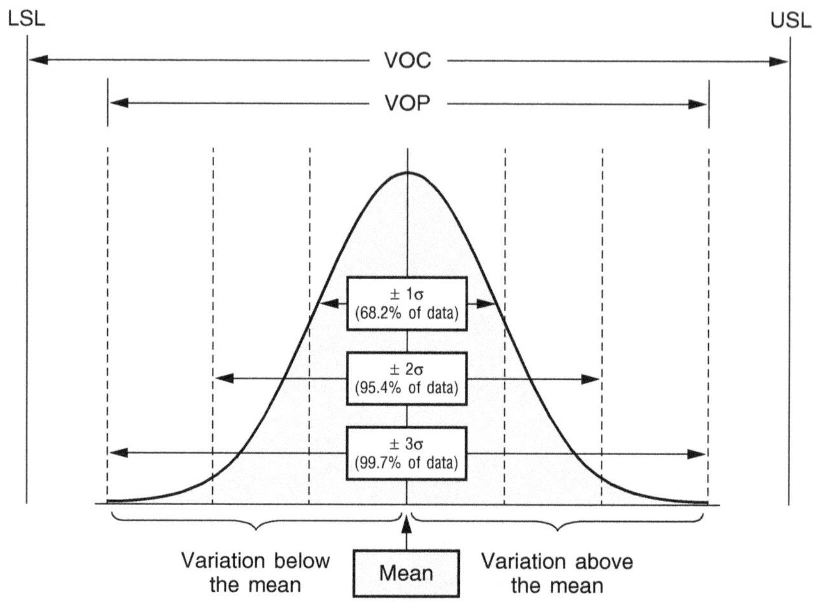

Figure 6.6 C_p = VOC/VOP.

process mean from the specification limits' midpoint, as shown in Figures 6.7 and 6.8.

C_p/C_{pk} shows short-term variation. P_p/P_{pk} shows long-term variation, which captures more special cause variation (Figure 6.9). It is for this reason that P_p/P_{pk} will always be lower than C_p/C_{pk}. C_{pk} and P_{pk} are the preferred methods for evaluating process capability since they both account for process location and width.

Though statistical software often shows capability indices as a part of the control chart graphic, it's important to understand that capability indices are not an element of control charts. Control charts (graphical) and capability indices (analytical), although complementary to one another, are two separate and distinct tools.

Now that we have covered the basics, let's talk about data review. As we review an organization's data analysis program, you want to ask, "What information is reviewed, by whom, and what are the data used for?" When looking at data, you want to look at more than it being within specification or control. You also want to understand trends in data. Understanding how to respond to uncontrolled conditions or negative trends is an often-overlooked portion of the less mature QMS.

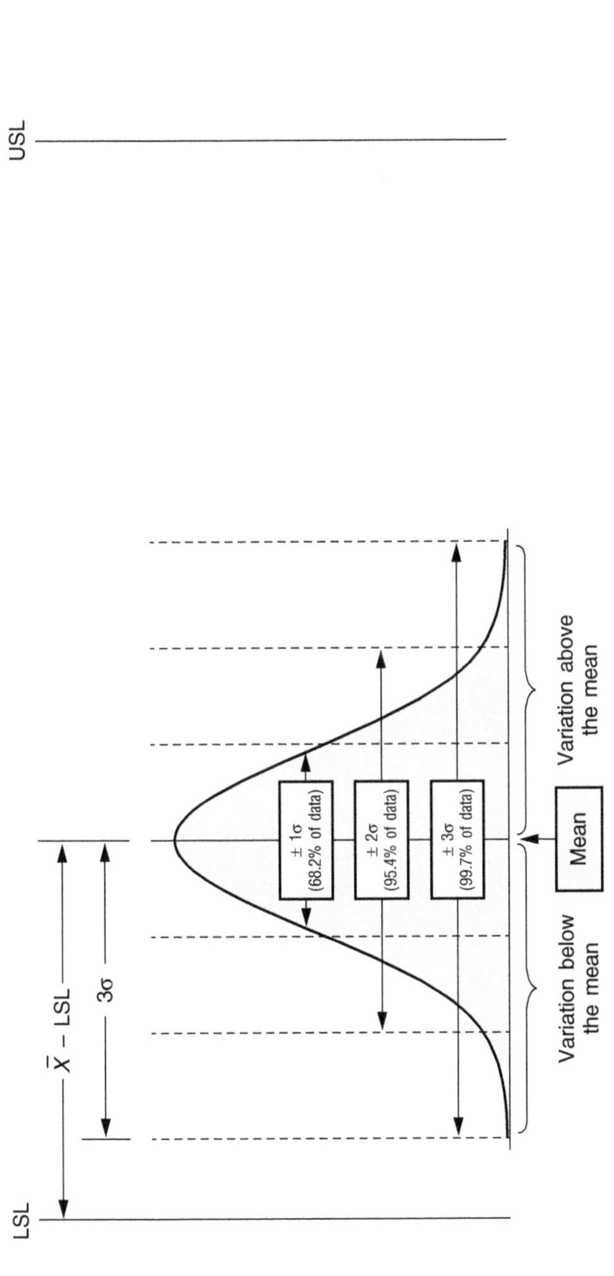

Figure 6.7 $C_{pk} = (\bar{X} - LSL)/3\sigma$.

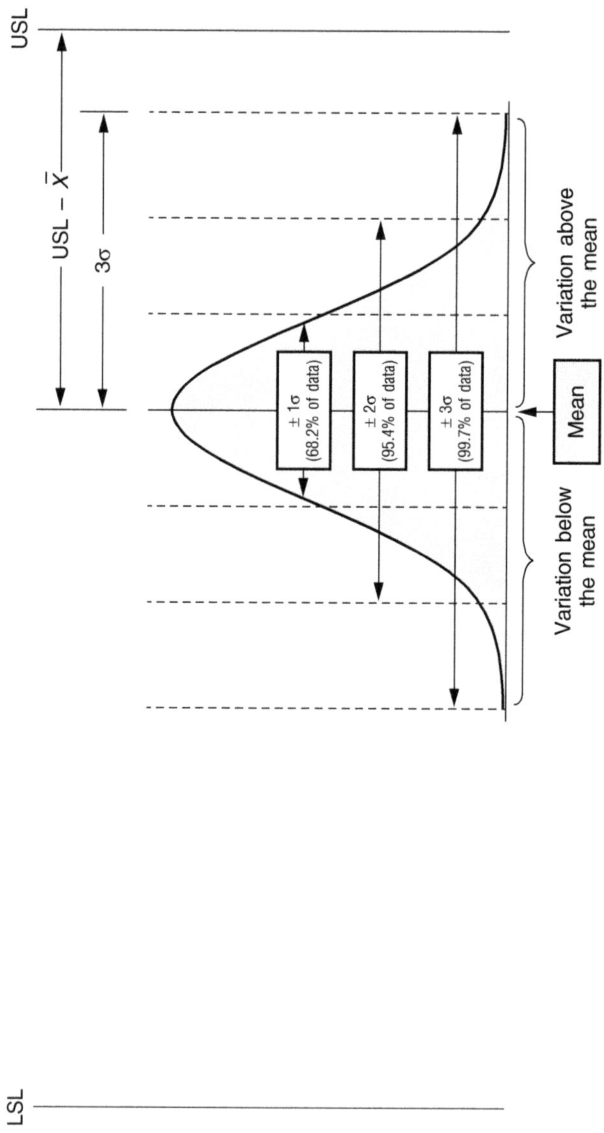

Figure 6.8 $C_{pk} = (USL - \bar{X})/3\sigma$.

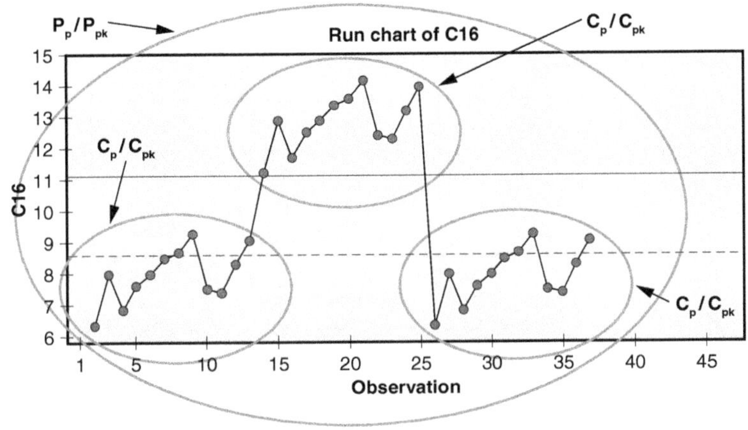

Number of runs about median:	8	Number of runs up or down:	15
Expected number of runs:	19.0	Expected number of runs:	23.7
Longest run about median:	13	Longest run up or down:	5
Approximate P-value for clustering:	0.000	Approximate P-value for trends:	0.000
Approximate P-value for mixtures:	1.000	Approximate P-value for oscillation:	1.000

Figure 6.9 Short-term versus long-term variation.

Decisions based on the analysis and evaluation of data and information are more likely to produce desired results.

—ISO 9000:2015 2.3.6.1

What does this mean to us? As auditors, we should be looking to confirm that the following maxim applies to the auditee's data analysis program:

- Don't collect data if you aren't going to plot it.
- Don't plot data if you aren't going to analyze it.
- Don't analyze data if you aren't going to do anything with the results.

Ideally, you would want to see process data evenly distributed around the process average as shown in Figure 6.10.

Some examples of commonly seen trends that would warrant further investigation are shown in Figures 6.11 through 6.14. You will note that some of these changes can be subtle, so you will need to be on the lookout for them.

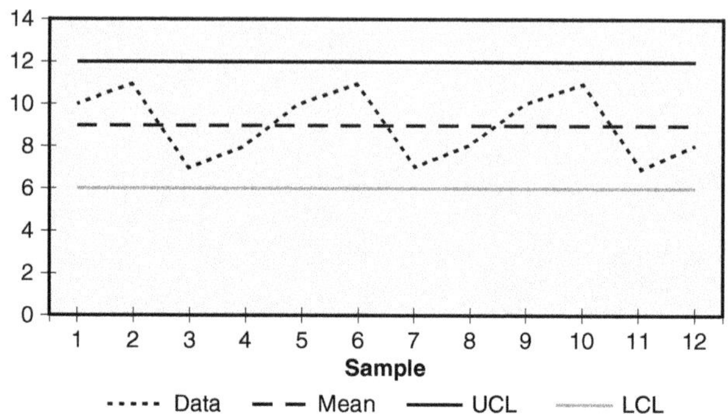

Figure 6.10 Control chart showing centered process.

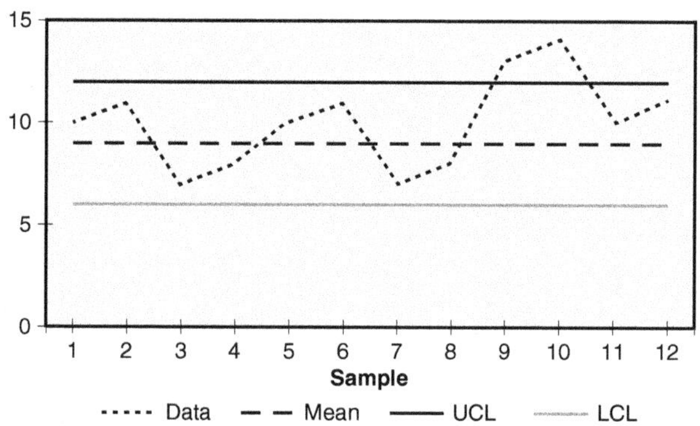

Figure 6.11 Control chart showing data upward shift.

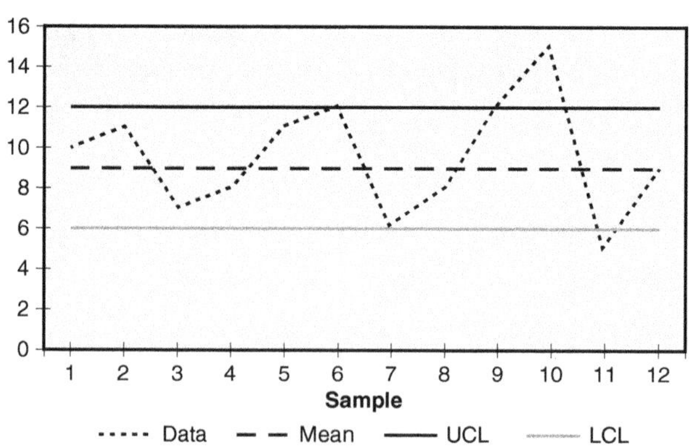

Figure 6.12 Increased variation.

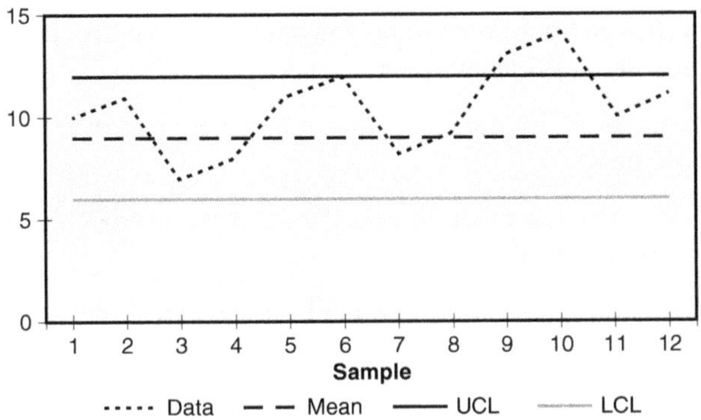

Figure 6.13 Control chart showing data trending upward.

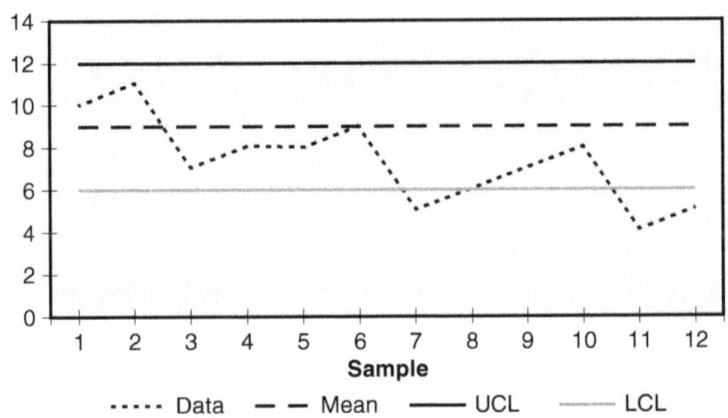

Figure 6.14 Control chart showing data trending downward.

There was a set of rules developed by Westinghouse in the 1980s called the *Westinghouse rules* that give additional examples of plotted data that might require investigation. However, you don't need to be a statistical expert and remember every guideline for when to launch an investigation based on data. You should, however, be able to recognize when there is the possibility of special cause variation indicated by plotted data and know what questions to ask.

Some of the questions that an auditor might ask when reviewing the process monitoring program are:

- What do you do when a negative trend is encountered?
- What do you do when an out-of-control condition is encountered?

- How do you know what to do when an out-of-control condition or adverse trend is encountered?
- If C_p/C_{pk} or P_p/P_{pk} data are captured, is there a minimum requirement?
- How do yields or other process data compare across shifts or between similar lines?
- Is there a structured program in place for review of and response to adverse trends/conditions in data?
- How do you identify positive trends that may point to an opportunity to transfer a best practice from one process or work center to another?
- What training is provided in SPC and data analysis?
- Are the daily metrics captured and aligned with organizational goals and objectives?
- How were the control or specification limits selected? Don't assume that a statistical, or even logical, method was used.

In our data-driven society, more data are available than ever before. It's important to not just understand the data that we are looking at, but to know which data to review. When looking at data analysis in an organization, it is important to understand how downward flow of strategic goals and objectives, as called out in ISO 9001:2015, is accomplished. It should be clear how operational targets support tactical objectives, which in turn support strategic goals. Each goal and objective should have an associated metric that will indicate when the goal or objective has been met. When there is not a clear link between goals, objectives, and metrics, it may sometimes be the case that unnecessary metrics are being tracked. Let's look at the following example of proper flow-down of corporate vision:

- *Vision*: Become marketplace leader within the next five years
- *Strategic goal*: Increased market share
  - *Metric*: Industry ranking
- *Tactical objective*: Improved quality
  - *Metrics*: Reduced customer return rate and increased customer satisfaction survey scores

- *Operational targets*: Reduce process variation
  - *Metric*: Lower scrap rate

We seek to derive insights from the review of data. Through those insights, data are transformed into information upon which decisions can be based. Reviewing data does not just occur by interpreting charts out on the manufacturing floor. Often, as part of an audit, we are called on to review validation reports. This may appear to be a daunting task. However, you do not have to have a degree in statistics or be a technical expert to provide a thorough review. Here are some basic tips:

- Is there an approved and released protocol?
- Are the data, which were specified in the protocol, in the report?
- Have all of the required signatories signed off on the report?
- Have all the success criteria been met?
- If all success criteria have not been met, were appropriate procedures followed?
- Any red lines crossed on the graphs? If so, what does that mean?

Auditors play an important role through their assessment of an organization's data analysis program. Understanding basic statistical tools and techniques will allow an experienced auditor to provide a thorough review regardless of their background.

In God we trust. All others please bring data.

—W. Edwards Deming

CASE IN POINT

"But the Screen Didn't Turn Red!": The Importance of Identifying and Responding to Negative Trends

In plastic injection molding, it is not uncommon for parts to be pulled for inspection and allowed to cool (in order for the part to finish shrinking while it cools) for a certain predetermined period of time before taking measurements. In the instance that we are about to discuss, the period of time that the parts were allowed to cool after being sampled was 24 hours. During this time, the job was allowed to continue running. In effect, Company UVW was "running at risk" for 24 hours because if inspection were to determine that the process had started producing nonconforming parts, then it would have been doing so for 24 hours. When you think about the fact that you may be producing hundreds of parts an hour, that is *a lot* of parts. This, however, was a known and accepted risk.

One day, an inspector noticed that though the parts being measured were acceptable, they were very close to the lower specification limit, and they had been getting closer and closer to that limit the last few days when she had taken measurements. It was at that point that she called the project quality engineer. The quality engineer investigated, and sure enough, they were making parts out of specification. Worse yet, many of the parts currently being inspected were out of specification. This meant that despite the fact that none of the cells on the inspection spreadsheet had "turned red" (indicating that a sampled part was out of specification), Company UVW had been making bad products for 24 hours (this happens to have been a long-running job). Upon further investigation, it was discovered that the data had been trending downward, as shown in Figure 6.15, for almost three months! No one had been paying attention. When area supervisors did their routine shift check and looked at the inspection spreadsheet, it was to verify that any "red cells" were being documented and investigated and make sure there was not a high count of red cells. It wasn't the inspector's fault. Nor was it the supervisor's. They both did what they were trained to do. The inspector measured parts to ensure that they met specification, and when

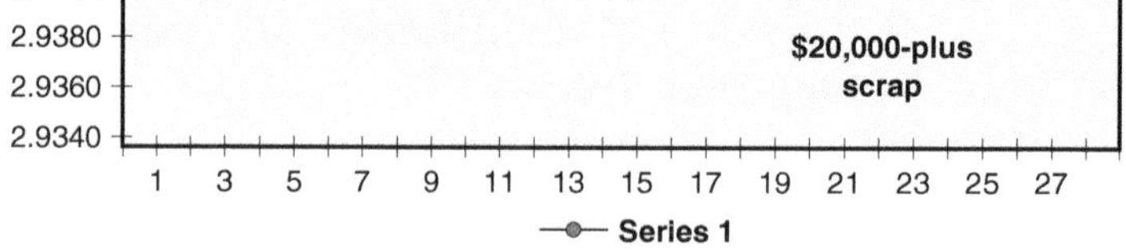

Figure 6.15 Negative trend resulting in $20,000 of scrap.

she noticed a potentially negative trend, she notified the appropriate quality engineer to investigate. The supervisor checked to ensure that there were no negative *out-of-specification* trends and that staff were responding appropriately when a product nonconformity was identified.

What the quality management system did *not* do was provide training or direction to look for graphical trends in data that were within specification, within control (at least for a while), and yet still displaying concerning behavior. This oversight resulted in a $20,000 dollar scrap loss, as shown in Figure 6.15.

Many companies have clearly defined roles, responsibilities, and expectations when it comes to responding to out-of-tolerance (OOT) or out-of-specification (OOS) situations. In fact, many quality regulations require them. What is not as common is providing training in basic statistical techniques to frontline employees and clear direction on how to respond to negative trends in data before parts begin to go out of specification or control. Such an oversight can cost you. Just ask Company UVW.

Conclusion

So, What Was This All About Anyway?

"You should understand and control your supplier's processes as if they were your own." That's what one notified body auditor said to me. Well, fat chance of that since there is only so much transparency you can have, and only so much control you can exert over a separate company. It is important to understand, though, that this is the "bar" that you have to set, the type of relationship that you must try to develop with your suppliers in order to flourish in this twenty-first century. A huge part of accomplishing this task is managing supply chain risk.

Risk-based auditing and the process approach really, really is "a thing." Risk-based auditing drives us to ask the right questions, allowing us to be proactive rather than reactive. For example, at one company using the Risk Is the Compass method of auditing created by Denis Devos, the question was asked during an audit of the shipping department "What are some of the risks that you face that could lead to you being unsuccessful in completing your duties? What could possibly go wrong here?" "Well, sometimes production will come out when no one from shipping is around and comingle scanned and unscanned parts." All the parts would have the same part number, be conforming, and packaged correctly, but by doing this it could lead to traceability issues due to the wrong parts being sent to the customer. In discussing this audit finding with management after the audit was complete, it was realized that this problem had occurred previously, but the company was unsure of what the cause had been. Such was not the case when this audit was being conducted, however.

The area process had been mapped, employees were trained and following relevant and current procedures. No problems, right? Well, if this had been a traditional compliance audit, that would have been the conclusion drawn. However, by taking risk into account as a potential process output—as a result of using the process approach while conducting the audit—the company was able to resolve the issue through an improvement project using the lean tools of 5S, layout, and standard work, as opposed to having to do a root cause investigation and implement corrective action after a problem had been identified at the customer. Proactive versus reactive.

While writing this book, I was reminded of how I was once engaged in a discussion about whether auditing is a skill set or a career. The answer is that it is both. The observation and analytical skills found in auditing can be useful at home as well as at work. The full auditing toolbox is a good one to have for anyone in management. Auditing can also be a rewarding career that pays well, where you can learn a lot, and that can take you around the world to places you would have never been otherwise. Mastering the best practices in auditing is important. It is equally important to master auditing soft skills and supporting technical skills, to communicate well, and to be culturally sensitive. Without *all* of these things, you may still be able to conduct a good audit, but you will not be a good auditor.

Consider learning a second language. Not only is this a good mental exercise contributing to a journey of lifelong learning, it could be a key discriminator between you and a competitor for a job that you are after in an increasingly global marketplace. The importance of having appropriate skills and credentials can't be underscored enough. Establishing credentials should just be a starting point, however. Read business journals and blog posts. Listen to podcasts beyond those related to your specific industry. This is how you identify global trends and understand emerging market needs in order to stay ahead of your individual competition.

FINAL THOUGHTS

This book, like any good audit, is meant to come to a conclusion based on a stated purpose. As I stated in my introduction to this work, "This book is meant to provide a detailed and useful discussion of the practical application of risk-based supplier auditing principles. It is also intended to be a primer for those new to the profession of supplier auditing, and to share tips and best practices that would benefit experienced auditors as well. These pages represent experience gained while conducting hundreds of domestic audits as well as audits conducted in six countries around the world over the course of a 20-plus-year career in auditing. I have tried to 'leave nothing on the table.'"

Does this book meet its stated purpose? Unlike an audit, it is up to you, the reader, and not the author of the written work, to draw that conclusion. Thank you for taking the time out of your lives to engage with me through my work. I hope that you have enjoyed the experience as much as I. I wish you warm regards and safe travels along your own audit trails.

Yours most sincerely,
Lance B. Coleman, Sr.

Appendix

ISO 19011:2018 User's Guide

ISO 19011:2018 *Guidelines for auditing management systems* provides the foundation for best auditing practices worldwide. Several hundred auditors, many with decades of auditing and quality management experience, came together from around the globe over the course of two years to contribute to the latest version of this standard. ISO 19011 is important because it forms the basis of auditing techniques for many certifications, such as the ASQ Certified Quality Auditor and Exemplar Global (as well as other auditor certifying bodies) Lead QMS Auditor certifications.

Most auditor certifications are a combination of bodies of knowledge—auditing tools and methods plus some additional ones. For industry-specific certifications, industry-specific requirements (whether regulatory or ISO or both) would be combined with auditing tools and techniques. For the ASQ Certified Quality Auditor designation, meant to allow auditors to audit successfully across multiple industries, auditing tools and techniques are combined with an in-depth study of quality tools, risk management, lean and Six Sigma, basic statistics, and so forth. In both of these cases, the methodology for employing auditing tools and techniques comes from ISO 19011.

The standard is well thought-out and provides its own "Cliff's Notes" for auditors who just want to use it as a quick reference guide. The content of ISO 19011:2018 is summarized in two process flow diagrams found in Figures 1 and 2 within the standard (see Figures A.1 and A.2). The top half of Figure 1 represents clause 5 and shows how an organization goes about establishing audit program guidelines, while the bottom half representing clause 6 shows the next level down, how to conduct an audit. Finally, Figure 2 provides detail on how to collect and verify evidence while conducting the audit. Figure 1 references the paragraphs within the standard where the reader can get further detail.

One significant change to the 2018 edition of the standard is a more in-depth discussion of addressing risks and opportunities for both the audit

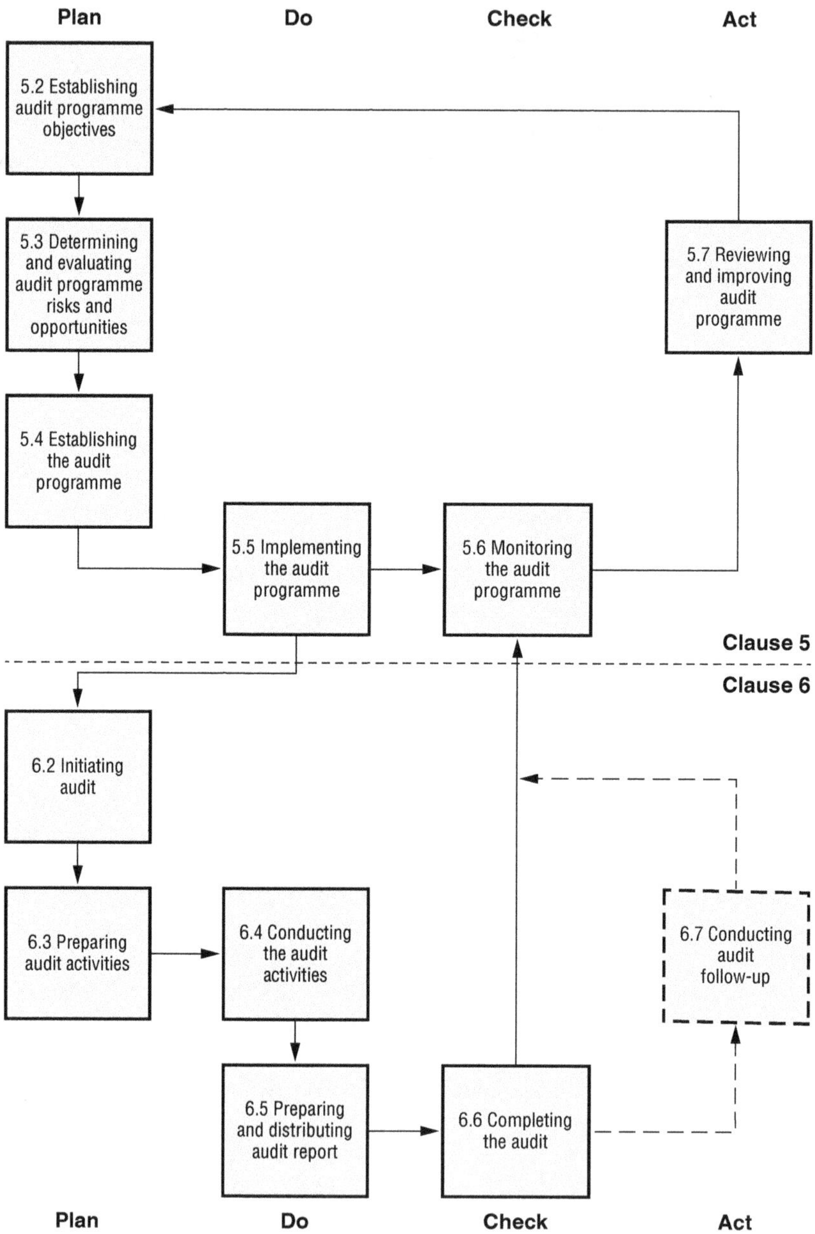

Note 1: This figure illustrates the application of the Plan–Do–Check–Act cycle in this document.

Note 2: Clause/subclause numbering refers to the relevant clauses/subclauses of this document.

Figure A.1 Process flow for the management of an audit program.

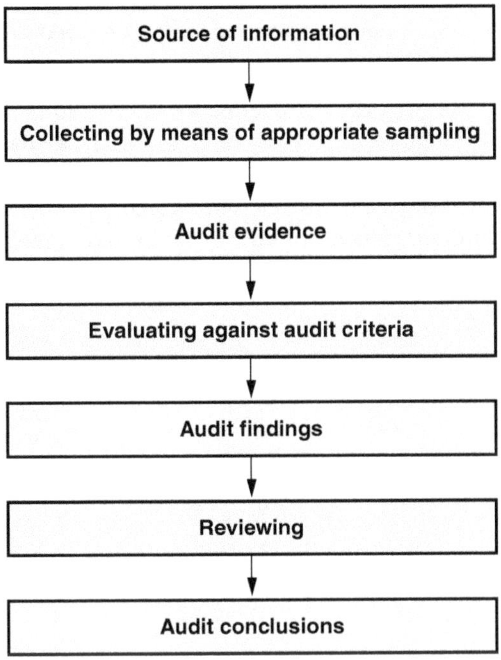

Figure A.2 Overview of the process of collecting and verifying information.

program and the quality management system that it is meant to monitor. As expected, there is the addition of the risk-based approach to the principles of auditing. Also, expansion of the guidance on managing an audit program, including audit program risk. New technologies are addressed as in the discussion on virtual auditing found in the annexes, which provide additional guidance for auditors regarding key topics. There are also updated requirements relating to audit plans, which are addressed as the output of the audit planning process.

ISO 19011 starts with scope, normative references, and terms and conditions, just like the related management system standards that this standard explains how to audit. After that, however, the section topics diverge to address the specifics of auditing as follows:

- Section 4 Principles of auditing
- Section 5 Managing an audit program
- Section 6 Conducting the audit
- Section 7 Competence and evaluation of auditors

- Annex A Additional guidance for auditors for planning and conducting audits

To recap, ISO 19011 provides a guideline for best auditing practices worldwide and is the foundation of most internationally recognized certified quality auditor bodies of knowledge. It can be used as a stand-alone auditor training manual or as a quick reference guide for experienced auditors, and is a worthwhile document for anyone interested in auditing to have in their library.

Glossary

audit—(1) Results of the evaluation of the collected audit evidence against audit criteria; (2) A systematic, independent, and documented process for obtaining audit evidence and evaluating it objectively to determine the extent to which audit criteria are fulfilled.

consumer risk—The risk of accepting something bad as good.

element method—The auditor examines each element of a standard or regulation to see how effectively it is implemented within the entire system.

hazard—Something found in the environment that is a potential source of harm, and that has a risk attached; typically a noun. For example, an extension cord stretched across a walkway would be a hazard. The risk attached would be that of tripping and falling. The harm would be the injury that might come from the fall.

process approach—The application of a system of processes within an organization, together with the identification and interactions of these processes, and their management, to produce a desired outcome.

producer risk—The risk of rejecting something good as bad

risk—The effects of uncertainty (on results).

risk-based thinking—A process that evaluates data inputs from the perspective of risk, with the output being a risk management program or model.

risk management—Coordinated activities to direct and control an organization with regard to risk.

risk tolerance—How willing a company is to accept risk in order to achieve a perceived benefit.

sole source—The only supplier from which you can acquire a particular product.

single source—Whereas there may be multiple places to acquire a particular product, this is the only supplier that has been qualified to provide it to you. Thus, replacement of this supplier could be costly in both time and expense.

supplier audit—On-site (supplier) verification activity, such as inspection or examination, of a process or quality system to ensure compliance to requirements.

supply chain—The global network used to deliver products and services—from raw materials to end customers—through an engineered flow of information, physical distribution, and cash.

supply chain management—The design, planning, execution, *control*, and *monitoring* of supply chain activities with the objective of creating net value, building a competitive infrastructure, leveraging worldwide logistics, synchronizing supply with demand, and measuring performance globally.

Bibliography

APICS. 2016. *Basics of Supply Chain Management: Participant Workbook.* Chicago: APICS.

Blanchard, Ken, and Jesse Lyn Stoner. 2011. *Full Steam Ahead! Unleash the Power of Vision in Your Work and Your Life.* San Francisco: Berrett-Koehler.

Durivage, Mark Allen. 2017. *The Certified Supplier Quality Professional Handbook.* Milwaukee: ASQ Quality Press.

Myerson, Paul. 2012. *Lean Supply Chain and Logistics Management.* New York: McGraw Hill.

Okes, Duke. 2013. *Performance Metrics: The Levers for Process Management.* Milwaukee: ASQ Quality Press.

Russell, J.P., editor. 2013. *The ASQ Auditing Handbook.* 4th ed. Milwaukee: ASQ Quality Press.

Russell, J.P., and Shauna Wilson. *eAuditing Fundamentals: Virtual Communication and Remote Auditing.* Milwaukee: ASQ Quality Press.

Index

A

B

C

D

E

F

G

H

I

J

K

L

M

N

O

P

R

S

T

V

W

Z

NOTES

NOTES

NOTES

NOTES

www.ingramcontent.com/pod-product-compliance
Lightning Source LLC
Chambersburg PA
CBHW071251180926
51613CB00001B/10
9780873899680